THE BEST SECRET OF GREATNESS

HOW HUMILITY LEADS TO HONOR, HARMONY, AND HAPPINESS

BY

SYAVIHA MULENGYA

This book is a gift

From:_____

To:_____

On:_____

Personal Comments

_____

_____

_____

_____

_____

Thank you God for your goodness, grace and the gift you have bestowed upon me

DEDICATION

- To my late parents, Samuel Mahamba and Elizabeth Vahingania, thank you for loving, listening and leading me in the ways of God.

- My brothers and sisters, Moise, Samson, Schandrack, Semu, Seriba, Yerusi, Desize, Kahambu and Katungu Mulengya, thank you for teaching me the values of hope, humility and hard work.

- To my mentors, Janine and Sid Phillips, thank you for your inspiration, instruction and information. You always encourage and believe in my vision.

- To Devin and Christine Walker, you have motivated me to serve, seek and stay close to God. Thank you for your wisdom and the great work you are doing.

- To my queen Rafiki Kavuya Syaviha, thank you for standing, supporting and serving with me in hard and good times. You are my miracle.

- To my lovely daughters, Blessed and Best and Brilliance, you always encourage, excite and enjoy my work. You are my greatest inspiration.

- To my friends and fans, you always advise, appreciate and assist me in this noble work. Thank you for the financial support.

Table of Content

Introduction

The Problem of Pride

Pride is a powerful poison that quietly corrupts the heart. It convinces people they are self-sufficient, superior, and beyond correction. Scripture warns us in **Proverbs 16:18**, *"Pride goes before destruction, and a haughty spirit before a fall."* Pride promotes division, discourages forgiveness, and prevents growth. It builds walls between people and blinds them to their own faults. In families, pride fuels arguments; in communities, it fosters conflict. Pride is the enemy of peace, the destroyer of unity, and the thief of wisdom. It whispers lies that we are better than others, that we don't need help, and that we deserve more. When pride rules, humility is silenced, and love is lost. The proud heart resists God's guidance and rejects His grace. Pride is not just a personal problem; it is a spiritual sickness. To heal, we must first recognize its presence and its power to pull us away from God and others.

Humility is the best cure for pride's poison. It begins with a heart that is teachable, tender, and truthful. **James 4:6** declares, *"God opposes the proud but gives grace to the humble."* Humility helps us hear correction without anger and accept help without shame. It softens the soul and strengthens the spirit. Humble people are not weak—they are wise. They know their limits, lean on God, and lift others up. Humility brings healing, harmony, and hope. It opens the door to deeper relationships and divine direction. When we walk humbly, we walk in step with God's will. Humility is

SYAVIHA MULENGYA

not thinking less of yourself—it's thinking of yourself less. It is the soil where love grows, peace blooms, and wisdom flourishes.

Jesus is the perfect picture of humility. Though He was divine, He chose to serve rather than be served. Philippians 2:8 says, "He humbled himself by becoming obedient to death—even death on a cross." He washed feet, welcomed sinners, and walked with the lowly. His humility was not weakness—it was wonder. Jesus showed that true greatness comes through grace, gentleness, and giving. He did not seek applause but offered compassion. He did not demand honor but delivered healing. His life teaches us that humility is the heart of heaven. When we follow Jesus, we learn to lead with love and live with purpose. His example encourages us to embrace humility as a lifestyle, not just a moment. Through Him, we see that humility is not just a virtue—it is victory.

Humility heals what pride harms. It restores broken relationships, rebuilds trust, and renews hearts. **Micah 6:8** reminds us, *"What does the Lord require of you? To act justly, to love mercy, and to walk humbly with your God."* Humility helps us forgive freely, listen deeply, and love sincerely. It teaches us to serve without seeking credit and to lead without craving control. In homes, humility brings harmony; in churches, it builds community. In workplaces, it strengthens collaboration and creativity. Humility is the bridge between brokenness and blessing. It is the path to peace, the road to reconciliation, and the key to spiritual strength. When humility is practiced, pride loses its power. The humble heart becomes a vessel for God's grace and a light in a dark world. Through humility, we find healing, hope, and holiness.

A humble life is a great life. It is marked by mercy, molded by grace, and moved by love. *Humility transforms how we think, speak,*

SYAVIHA MULENGYA

and serve. It turns selfishness into selflessness and bitterness into blessing. The humble person seeks God's glory, not their own gain. They live with purpose, walk with peace, and lead with patience. Humility invites joy, inspires generosity, and ignites faith. It is the foundation of lasting relationships and the fuel for spiritual growth. When we choose humility, we choose to reflect Christ. We become more compassionate, more courageous, and more connected to God. Humility is not just a choice—it is a calling. Let us embrace it daily, and watch how God uses it to shape us into vessels of His love and light.

1

Why Humility Matters So Much

Humility is often mistaken for weakness, but it is one of the greatest strengths a person can carry. It doesn't mean thinking less of yourself—it means thinking of yourself less often. A humble heart is open, honest, and hungry to grow. It listens before it speaks, learns before it leads, and loves without limits. Humility helps us handle life with grace, not pride. It softens the soul and strengthens the spirit. **Proverbs 22:4** says, *"Humility is the fear of the Lord; its wages are riches and honor and life."* That means when we walk humbly with God, we walk into blessing. ***Humility opens the door to peace, wisdom, and deeper relationships. It helps us hold truth gently and treat others kindly.*** A humble person doesn't need to be perfect—they need to be present. And in that presence, they find purpose. Humility matters because it makes room for what truly matters.

Humility brings honor—not the kind that shouts, but the kind that shines. People admire those who are gentle, gracious, and grounded. A proud person may demand attention, but a humble person earns respect. They don't push their way forward—they pull others up. Think of a leader who listens, lifts, and lets others shine. That kind of leadership lasts. Jesus said, *"Whoever humbles himself will be exalted"* (**Matthew 23:12**). Honor doesn't come from loud words—it comes from quiet strength. Humility helps us handle praise without pride and criticism without collapse. It teaches us to celebrate others and serve without seeking credit. True honor is not about being seen—it's about being sincere. And when we live humbly, honor follows like a shadow in sunlight. Humility doesn't lower your value—it lifts your legacy.

Humility creates **harmony** where pride causes pain. In homes, friendships, and communities, humble hearts heal what pride breaks. Harmony happens when people choose peace over power. A humble person says, "I'm sorry," and means it. They listen to understand, not just to reply. Imagine two friends in conflict—one chooses humility, and the fight fades. That's the power of a soft answer and a willing heart. Humility helps us forgive quickly and love deeply. It holds relationships together when pride would tear them apart. *Harmony isn't about agreeing on everything—it's about honoring each other through everything.* Humble people don't need to win every argument—they want to keep every connection. And in that choice, harmony grows. Where humility lives, peace follows.

Humility leads to **happiness**—not the kind that fades, but the kind that fills. A humble person doesn't chase applause—they choose appreciation. They find joy in helping, not in being noticed. Humility hushes the hunger for more and highlights the beauty of enough. It helps us live with gratitude, not greed. Think of someone who serves quietly, smiles often, and gives freely. Their joy isn't loud—but it's lasting. Humility helps us see blessings in small things and find peace in simple moments. It teaches us that happiness isn't found in being first—it's found in being faithful. *Humble hearts are light—they don't carry the heavy weight of pride.* They laugh more, love more, and live with less stress. Happiness doesn't come from having everything—it comes from holding everything with grace. And humility is the key that unlocks that joy.

Finally, humility brings **healing**—deep, lasting, and life-giving. It heals broken hearts, broken homes, and broken hopes. Humility helps us admit our pain and ask for help. It opens the door to grace and closes the door to shame. When we humble ourselves before God, He lifts us up with love. When we humble ourselves before others, **they feel safe, seen, and supported. Healing begins when pride ends. Humility helps us forgive what hurt us and release what holds us back.** It teaches us to be gentle with ourselves and generous with others. Healing isn't just about fixing what's broken—it's about growing something new. Humble hearts don't hide—they heal. And in that healing, we find strength, peace, and joy. Because humility isn't just a virtue—it's a vessel for transformation.

1. Humility Leads to Honor

Humility is one of the most powerful secrets to achieving true greatness. It begins with recognizing that we are not perfect and that growth is a lifelong journey. A humble heart accepts correction, seeks wisdom, and welcomes change. This attitude opens doors to peace, purpose, and progress. The Bible reminds us in **Proverbs 11:2**, *"When pride comes, then comes disgrace, but with humility comes wisdom."* Humility helps us learn from others and appreciate their strengths without feeling threatened. It teaches us to serve rather than seek status, and to lift others up instead of pushing ourselves forward. Jesus modeled this perfectly, saying in **Matthew 20:26**, *"Whoever wants to become great among you must be your* *servant."* True greatness is not loud—it's loving. It's not about being first—it's about being faithful. Humility helps us grow in character, not just in achievement. And in that growth, we find grace. Greatness begins where pride ends.

Honor is not about applause—it's about authenticity. It is earned through integrity, not demanded through ego. Humility lays the foundation for honor by creating space for respect to grow. When we admit we don't have all the answers, we show wisdom. When we value others' voices, we show strength. **James 4:10** says, *"Humble yourselves before the Lord, and He will lift you up."* That lifting is not just spiritual—it's relational. People trust those who are honest, kind, and humble. They follow leaders who listen and care. Honor flows naturally when humility is present. It doesn't need to be chased—it arrives quietly, clothed in grace. **Proverbs 15:33** adds, *"Humility comes before honor."* When we walk humbly, we walk with dignity. And in that walk, we earn the kind of respect that lasts.

Humility transforms how we relate to others. It softens our words, opens our ears, and strengthens our hearts. In families, friendships, and communities, humility is the glue that holds people together. It helps us forgive quickly, speak gently, and love deeply. **Colossians 3:12** encourages us to *"clothe yourselves with compassion, kindness, humility, gentleness and patience."* Humble people don't compete—they connect. They don't dominate—they collaborate. This attitude creates harmony, trust, and unity. It turns conflict into conversation and pride into partnership. Humility helps us see others not as rivals, but as teammates. And in that spirit of togetherness, greatness grows—not through force, but through faithfulness. Where humility lives, peace follows.

Humility is the quiet force behind lasting success. It keeps us grounded when we rise and graceful when we fall. It reminds us that greatness is not about being above others—it's about being among them. **Micah 6:8** says, *"What does the Lord require of you? To act justly, to love mercy, and to walk humbly with your God."* Humility leads to honor because it reflects a heart that is wise, willing, and worthy. It teaches us to serve with joy, lead with love, and live with purpose. When we walk humbly, we walk freely— unburdened by ego, open to growth, and full of grace. The world may celebrate pride, but heaven honors humility. **Proverbs 18:12** reminds us, *"Before a downfall the heart is proud, but humility comes before honor."* And in that sacred space, we discover that the true path to greatness is not paved with glory, but with grace. Humility matters because it makes us better—not just in what we do, but in who we become.

2. Humility Leads to Harmony

Harmony is essential for a peaceful and fulfilling life. Whether in families, friendships, or communities, harmony allows people to live together with understanding and respect. It brings calm to conflict, unity to diversity, and strength to relationships. But harmony doesn't happen by accident—it grows from the choices we make every day. One of the most powerful choices is humility. When we choose to be humble, we open the door to deeper connection. Humility helps us see others not as competitors, but as companions. It softens our words, opens our ears, and strengthens our hearts. In a world that often celebrates pride, humility becomes a quiet force for peace. It helps us live with grace, not judgment. And where humility leads, harmony follows. Because when people feel heard and honored, peace begins to bloom.

SYAVIHA MULENGYA

Humility helps us understand and connect with others. It teaches us to set aside pride and selfishness, making room for empathy and compassion. A humble person listens—not just to respond, but to truly understand. They value others' thoughts, feelings, and experiences. This attitude builds bridges instead of walls. It allows us to relate to people from different backgrounds and beliefs. Humility helps us say, "I may not know everything, but I'm willing to learn." It invites kindness, patience, and respect into every conversation. When we are humble, we don't need to win every argument—we want to keep every relationship. This mindset creates a safe space where people feel seen and supported. And in that space, harmony grows stronger. Because humility doesn't push—it welcomes.

The Bible speaks clearly about the power of humility in relationships. In **Philippians 2:3-4**, we are told, "Do nothing out of selfish ambition or vain conceit. Rather, in humility value others above yourselves, not looking to your own interests but each of you to the interests of the others." This verse reminds us that humility is not weakness—it's wisdom. It's the choice to lift others up, even when we could focus on ourselves. When we follow this teaching, we create communities built on care, not competition. Humility helps us work together, share burdens, and celebrate each other's victories. It turns strangers into friends and neighbors into family. The more we practice humility, the more we reflect the heart of Christ. And in doing so, we build relationships that last. Because humility doesn't divide—it unites.

Humility also strengthens trust and cooperation. When people feel respected and valued, they are more willing to work together. Humble hearts don't seek control—they seek connection. They don't demand attention—they offer support. This creates a culture of teamwork, where everyone's voice matters. In families,

SYAVIHA MULENGYA

humility helps parents and children grow closer. In friendships, it helps people forgive and move forward. In communities, it helps leaders serve with integrity and citizens live with dignity. Humility builds trust because it shows that we care more about people than power. It helps us handle disagreements with grace and find common ground. And when trust is strong, harmony becomes natural. Because humility doesn't compete—it cooperates.

Humility is the foundation of harmony. It helps us live with purpose, love with patience, and lead with kindness. Humility reminds us that we are all learning, growing, and worthy of respect. It teaches us to celebrate others, not just ourselves. When humility fills our hearts, harmony fills our homes, schools, churches, and communities. It creates a world where people feel safe, supported, and seen. And that kind of world begins with one humble choice at a time. The Bible shows us that humility is not just a virtue—it's a way of life. A life that brings peace, unity, and joy to everyone it touches. Because humility doesn't just change how we act—it changes how we live. And in that change, harmony finds a home.

3. Humility Leads to Happiness

Happiness is often misunderstood as something earned through success, wealth, or recognition. Many chase achievements, hoping they will bring lasting joy, only to find that satisfaction fades quickly. True happiness, however, is not found in possessions or praise—it is found within. It grows from a heart that is content, peaceful, and free from the need to impress. Humility plays a powerful role in this inner joy. When we let go of pride and comparison, we release the pressure to prove ourselves. Humility helps us appreciate the present moment and the people around us. It shifts our focus from chasing more to cherishing what we already have. Simple joys—like a quiet walk, a heartfelt conversation, or a moment of stillness—become sources of deep happiness. Humility teaches us that we don't need to be noticed to be fulfilled. And in that quiet freedom, happiness begins to bloom. **Proverbs 22:4 —** *"Humility is the fear of the Lord; its wages are riches and honor and life."* This verse reminds us that humility leads not only to peace but also to a life filled with true reward—rich in meaning, honor, and joy.

Humility helps you find happiness by teaching you to appreciate yourself as you are and to value others without comparison. You begin to understand that life is not a race, and your worth isn't measured by being better than someone else. Humility quiets the voice of pride and opens your heart to grace. It allows you to celebrate others without feeling threatened and to love yourself without needing applause. As you embrace humility, you stop chasing after approval and start living with gratitude. You begin to notice the blessings that were always there—family, friendship, faith, and peace. Humility teaches you to live simply and love deeply. It replaces competition with compassion and comparison with connection. In this way, happiness becomes a steady presence rather than a fleeting feeling. **Matthew 5:5 —** *"Blessed are the meek, for they will inherit the earth."* This verse shows that gentleness and humility are not signs of weakness—they are the keys to receiving lasting peace and spiritual reward.

By focusing on humility, you build a deeper kind of satisfaction—one that success alone cannot offer. External achievements may bring temporary excitement, but they rarely bring lasting peace. Humility invites you to let go of pride and embrace authenticity. It encourages you to live kindly, speak gently, and act with sincerity. When you prioritize inner values over outward appearances, you begin to experience a happiness that endures. Humble people find joy in being real, not in being admired.

SYAVIHA MULENGYA

They live with purpose, not performance. This kind of happiness is rooted in character, not circumstance. It grows stronger through trials and shines brighter in quiet moments. Humility helps you stay grounded, even when life feels uncertain. And in that grounding, you find peace that cannot be shaken. **Psalm 37:11** — *"But the meek will inherit the land and enjoy peace and prosperity."* This verse reinforces that humility leads to a life filled with peace, stability, and joy—not just temporary success.

Humility is more than a virtue—it's a way to live with joy and meaning. It frees you from the weight of pride and opens your heart to grace. Humility teaches you to love without limits, to serve without seeking credit, and to live without fear of judgment. It helps you see beauty in simplicity and strength in gentleness. When you walk humbly, you walk freely. You stop striving for happiness and start living in it. The world may tell you to chase more, but humility tells you to cherish what matters most. And in that quiet wisdom, you find a happiness that lasts—not because of what you have, but because of who you've become. **Philippians 4:11** — *"I have learned to be content whatever the circumstances."* Paul's words remind us that true happiness comes from a humble heart that finds peace in every season—not from external success.

4. Humility Leads Healing

Healing—whether emotional, physical, or spiritual—begins with a heart that is open and willing. It requires us to set aside pride and admit that we may need help, support, or guidance. This first step is often the hardest, yet it is also the most powerful. Humility allows us to say, "I can't do this alone," and invites others to walk beside us. It softens our defenses and opens our minds to new perspectives. When we are humble, we become teachable, receptive, and ready to grow. This posture creates an environment where healing can flourish. Pride isolates, but humility connects. It builds bridges between people and fosters trust. Healing happens faster and deeper when we allow others to care for us. The Bible reminds us in **Proverbs 11:2**, *"When pride comes, then comes disgrace, but with humility comes wisdom."* Wisdom is often the first step toward healing—and humility is the path that leads us there.

The story of Naaman the leper is a powerful example of humility's role in healing. Naaman was a respected military commander, yet he suffered from a disease he could not cure. His pride initially kept him from accepting the prophet Elisha's simple instructions to wash in the Jordan River. But when he humbled himself and obeyed, he was miraculously healed (**2 Kings 5:1-14**). His transformation didn't come through status or strength—it came through surrender. Naaman's healing was not just physical; it was also spiritual and emotional. He learned that true power lies in obedience and humility. His story reminds us that healing often requires letting go of our own expectations and trusting a higher wisdom. When we humble ourselves, we open the door to restoration. And in that surrender, we find strength we didn't know we had.

Humility not only helps us accept help—it teaches us how to live in community. It reminds us that we are not meant to carry burdens alone. When we let go of pride, we make space for others to support, encourage, and walk with us. This shared journey builds trust and deepens relationships. Humility teaches us to listen, to learn, and to lean on others without shame. It helps us grow through connection rather than isolation. Healing becomes more than a personal process—it becomes a shared experience. As we open our hearts, we discover the beauty of mutual care and compassion. The wisdom gained through humility strengthens not just the individual but the entire community. And in that strength, healing becomes a collective victory.

In the end, humility is not just a step toward healing—it is the soil in which wholeness grows. It helps us face challenges with grace and respond to pain with patience. Humility allows us to be honest about our struggles and hopeful about our future. It teaches us to value progress over perfection and to embrace the journey, not just the destination. When we live humbly, we live freely—unburdened by ego and open to grace. Healing flows more easily when we stop pretending to be strong and start allowing ourselves to be real. The Bible encourages this posture in **James 4:10:** *"Humble yourselves before the Lord, and He will lift you up."* That lifting is not just physical—it's emotional, spiritual, and relational. Through humility, we find the courage to heal and the strength to rise.

5. Humility Leads to Helping Others

True leadership is rooted in humility. A humble leader is one who serves others and leads by example. They are not driven by ego or the need for power but by a genuine desire to help others succeed. This type of leadership inspires loyalty and respect. As Jesus taught in **Matthew 20:26-28,** *"Whoever wants to become great among you must be your servant, and whoever wants to be first must be your slave—just as the Son of Man did not come to be served, but to serve, and to give his life as a ransom for many."* Humble leadership creates a positive environment where everyone can thrive.

Humility is a key ingredient in the recipe for greatness. By embracing humility, you can achieve honor, harmony, happiness, and healing. In the following chapters, we will delve deeper into each of these aspects and discover how humility can unlock your true potential. Remember, as **1 Peter 5:6** encourages us, *"Humble yourselves, therefore, under God's mighty hand, that he may lift you up in due time."* Embrace humility, and you will find that it opens doors to a life of true greatness.

2

Know The Best Secret

What is Humility?

1. Recognize Your Strengths and Weaknesses

Humility starts with self-awareness. It means recognizing both your strengths and weaknesses. Knowing what you are good at helps you use your talents effectively, while understanding your limitations allows you to seek help and improve. As **Romans 12:3** advises, *"Do not think of yourself more highly than you ought, but rather think of yourself with sober judgment."*

2. Rely on God

Humility involves trusting in God and seeking His guidance. It means acknowledging that you cannot do everything on your own and that you need divine support. This trust helps you stay grounded and focused on what truly matters. **Proverbs 3:5-6** encourages us, *"Trust in the Lord with all your heart and lean not on your own understanding; in all your ways submit to him, and he will make your paths straight."*

3. Reason with Others

Humility is an essential quality that promotes meaningful dialogue and reasoning with others. It involves a willingness to listen to different perspectives without judgment and to value others' opinions as much as your own. When you approach conversations with humility, you create an environment where ideas can be exchanged freely and respectfully. This openness to discussion not only helps in solving problems but also strengthens relationships by building trust and understanding. A humble attitude ensures that everyone feels heard and valued, paving the way for constructive, harmonious interactions.

Isaiah 1:18 says, "Come now, let us reason together, says the Lord." Coming together with an open heart to seek common ground is a good thing. When we practice humility, we put aside selfish pride and focus on collective wisdom. By being open to reasoning and dialogue, we learn from others and grow in ways we may not have expected. Ultimately, humility develops mutual respect, strengthens relationships, and creates a foundation for peace and unity in both personal and community relationships.

4. Remind Yourself of Your Past

Humility is about staying grounded and remembering your origins. It encourages you to reflect on the journey that brought you to where you are today and to appreciate the experiences that shaped your character. No matter how successful or bright your present may be, humility reminds you to remain grateful for the lessons learned along the way. By acknowledging the struggles, sacrifices, and blessings of your past, you foster a deeper sense of gratitude and connection to your roots. As **Deuteronomy 8:2** says, *"Remember how the Lord your God led you all the way in the wilderness these forty years."* Humility is also about recognizing God's guidance and grace in your life. When you honor your past with gratitude, you create a foundation for growth and authenticity. Humility helps you remain true to yourself while valuing the journey that made you who you are.

5. Respect People

Humility is about showing kindness and respect to others, recognizing their worth, and valuing their contributions. When we treat people with humility, we create an environment filled with positivity and support, where everyone feels appreciated. It's not about putting ourselves down but lifting others up, creating space for cooperation and harmony. As **Philippians 2:3-4** reminds us, *"Do nothing out of selfish ambition or vain conceit. Rather, in humility value others above yourselves."* This attitude helps build stronger relationships, fosters trust, and brings out the best in everyone, leading to a more peaceful and united community.

6. Respond Well and React with Wisdom

Humility means handling situations with wisdom and calmness. Instead of reacting quickly, take a moment to think before you respond. This helps you better handle challenges and stay in control of your emotions. When you answer calmly and with understanding, you can bring peace to tough situations. As **Proverbs 15:1** says, *"A gentle answer turns away wrath, but a harsh word stirs up anger."* Choosing humility and gentle words can stop fights and help build stronger and more peaceful relationships.

7. Resist Pride

Humility is about staying true to yourself and resisting the temptation to become proud or arrogant, no matter how successful you become. It reminds us that success should not make us forget our values or where we came from. Pride can often lead to mistakes and even failure, while humility helps us stay grounded and focused on improving ourselves. By choosing humility, we remain open to learning and growing, even when we achieve great things. As **Proverbs 16:18** wisely warns, *"Pride goes before destruction, a haughty spirit before a fall."* This serves as a reminder that humility is not just a virtue—it is a safeguard that keeps us on the path to lasting success and fulfillment.

What Humility is Not

1. Humility Is Not Insecurity

Humility is not weakness—it's quiet strength. Being humble doesn't mean you doubt your worth or shrink back in fear. True humility comes from knowing who you are and being confident without needing to prove it. A humble person doesn't boast or seek constant approval because they are secure in their identity. They recognize their own gifts but also celebrate the strengths of others. This balance creates a spirit of kindness, not competition. Humility allows you to lead with grace and walk with wisdom. It's not about hiding your light—it's about letting it shine without casting shadows on others. Insecurity seeks validation; humility offers value. When you are truly humble, you don't need to be loud to be heard. You speak through your actions, and your character speaks for itself. Humility is not self-doubt—it's self-awareness wrapped in quiet confidence.

2. Humility Is Not Indecisiveness

Humility doesn't mean you're unsure or afraid to make decisions. In fact, humble people often make the wisest choices because they listen, reflect, and act with care. They consider others' perspectives, but they don't lose their own voice. A humble person can stand firm when needed and lead with clarity. They don't rush to judgment, but they don't avoid responsibility either. Humility brings balance—it allows you to be open without being passive. It's the strength to say "I don't know" and the courage to say "I believe this is right." Humble leaders make thoughtful decisions that serve others, not just themselves. They don't seek control—they seek what's best. Indecisiveness is rooted in fear; humility is rooted in wisdom. When humility guides your choices, you lead with purpose and peace.

3. Humility Is Not Ignorance

Humility is not about lacking knowledge—it's about being open to more. A humble person doesn't pretend to know everything; they're eager to learn. They ask questions, seek understanding, and welcome correction. Humility says, "I have something to offer, and I have something to learn." It's the mindset that fuels growth and deepens wisdom. Ignorance closes doors; humility opens them wide. A truly humble person listens more than they speak and learns more than they assume. They know that wisdom begins with curiosity and grows through experience. Humility helps us admit when we're wrong and grow from it. It's not blind acceptance—it's thoughtful awareness. When we embrace humility, we become lifelong learners, always growing, always improving. And that kind of learning leads to lasting impact.

4. Humility Is Not Irresponsibility

Humility doesn't avoid responsibility—it embraces it. A humble person owns their actions and accepts the consequences. They don't blame others or make excuses—they step up and make things right. Humility means saying, "I made a mistake," and then doing the work to fix it. It's not about being perfect—it's about being accountable. Irresponsibility avoids the hard truths; humility faces them with grace. A humble heart doesn't run from challenges—it rises to meet them. It values integrity over image and growth over comfort. When you're humble, you take responsibility not just for yourself, but for how your actions affect others. You lead with honesty, and you live with purpose. Humility doesn't weaken your character—it strengthens it.

5. Humility Is Not Impulsiveness

Humility is thoughtful, not reckless. It teaches us to pause, reflect, and act with intention. A humble person doesn't rush into decisions—they consider the impact. They think before they speak and weigh their choices with care. Impulsiveness reacts; humility responds. It brings patience into moments of pressure and wisdom into moments of emotion. Humility helps us avoid regret by guiding us with clarity and calm. It's not about hesitation—it's about discernment. A humble heart seeks peace, not drama. It chooses what's right over what's easy. When humility leads, our actions reflect purpose, not impulse. And in that purpose, we find peace, strength, and direction.

Why Humility Is The Best Secret

1. Builds

Humility builds strong foundations for personal growth and meaningful relationships. When you choose to be humble, you create a space where trust, respect, and kindness can thrive. It helps you grow with grace and develop in a healthy, positive way. Humility allows you to learn from others, admit mistakes, and stay open to change. It keeps your heart soft and your mind teachable. As **Proverbs 22:4** says, *"Humility is the fear of the Lord; its wages are riches and honor and life."* This means that when we walk humbly with God, we receive blessings that go far beyond material things. Humility builds character, deepens faith, and strengthens every part of life.

2. Bridges

Humility acts like a bridge—it brings people together. When you are humble, you listen with care and speak with respect. You value others' thoughts and feelings, even when they differ from your own. This attitude creates unity, not division. Humility helps us move from selfishness to selflessness, from isolation to connection. **Philippians 2:3-4** reminds us, *"Do nothing out of selfish ambition or vain conceit. Rather, in humility value others above yourselves."* When we live this way, we build stronger relationships filled with peace, understanding, and love. Humility doesn't just connect people—it heals them.

3. Balances

Humility brings balance to your life. It keeps you grounded when things go well and hopeful when things go wrong. It helps you celebrate success without becoming proud and face failure without losing heart. Humility reminds you that growth is a journey, not a race. It teaches you to stay focused on learning and improving, rather than seeking praise. **Proverbs 11:2** says, *"When pride comes, then comes disgrace, but with humility comes wisdom."* Wisdom helps you stay steady, even in uncertain times. Humility keeps your feet on the ground and your heart in the right place.

4. Benefits

Humility brings benefits to you and everyone around you. It creates a positive atmosphere where kindness, support, and encouragement flow freely. When you are humble, people feel safe with you—they're more willing to help, share, and grow together. Humility builds trust and invites cooperation. **James 4:10** says, *"Humble yourselves before the Lord, and He will lift you up."* God honors those who walk humbly, and others do too. The benefits of humility are seen in stronger friendships, healthier communities, and a deeper sense of peace.

5. Bears

Humility bears with others in love and patience. It means walking alongside people in their struggles, not judging them for their flaws. A humble person doesn't point fingers—they offer a helping hand. They encourage, support, and guide others with compassion. Humility understands that everyone has weaknesses and that grace is more powerful than criticism. It creates a safe space for growth and healing. When we bear with one another in humility, we build relationships rooted in mutual respect and care. We lift each other up and grow stronger together.

6. Boosts

Humility boosts others by celebrating their success and cheering them on. It finds joy in lifting people up, not in competing with them. A humble person gives sincere compliments, offers encouragement, and helps others reach their potential. They don't need the spotlight—they shine by helping others shine. Humility boosts confidence, builds morale, and strengthens unity. It creates a culture of kindness where everyone feels valued. When we choose humility, we build people up instead of tearing them down—and that makes all the difference.

7. Blesses

Humility blesses everyone it touches. It inspires others through gentle words, kind actions, and a heart that puts others first. A humble person brings peace into every room and hope into every heart. They make people feel seen, accepted, and loved. Humility speaks life, prays for others, and wishes them well. It doesn't seek attention—it seeks to uplift. **Philippians 2:3-4** reminds us again, *"In* *humility, value others above yourselves."* When we live this way, we become a blessing to the world around us. Humility is a quiet force that brings light, love, and lasting change.

3

Secret to Greatness

God did not create you to be ordinary or aimless—He placed greatness within you for a divine purpose. You were not called to be passive or invisible, but to serve with compassion, stand with conviction, and speak with grace. Scripture affirms this in **Ephesians 2:10**: *"For we are God's workmanship, created in Christ Jesus to do good works, which God prepared in advance for us to do."* This means your life is not random—it's designed for impact. Consider Joseph, who served faithfully in prison before rising to power in Egypt. His greatness wasn't in his title, but in his unwavering trust and integrity. When you set a good example, speak kindly, and show others the way, you reflect the heart of Christ, who said, *"Let your light shine before others, that they may see your good deeds and glorify your Father in heaven"* (**Matthew 5:16**).

True greatness is not measured by applause or recognition, but by how you respond to the needs around you. When you solve problems with wisdom, seek God earnestly, and set people free from fear, shame, or confusion, you embody the mission of Jesus. **Luke 4:18** declares, *"He has sent me to proclaim freedom for the* *prisoners and recovery of sight for the blind, to set the oppressed free."* You are called to be a liberator—not necessarily in grand gestures, but in everyday acts of love and truth. Think of Moses, who doubted his ability but led a nation out of bondage because he trusted God's voice. Or Esther, who risked her life to save her people. Their greatness was revealed in obedience, courage, and service. When you share generously, forgive freely, and walk humbly, you become a vessel of God's power and compassion.

Greatness also grows through spiritual discipline and personal development. Seeking God daily, studying His Word, and stewarding your gifts are not just religious habits—they are the building blocks of a life that honors Him. **Philippians 2:3-4** teaches, *"Do nothing out of selfish ambition or vain conceit. Rather, in humility value others above yourselves."* This kind of greatness is quiet but powerful—it transforms families, communities, and even nations. David, though flawed, was called a man after God's own heart because he repented, worshiped, and led with passion. When you stretch beyond your comfort zone, sharpen your skills, and strengthen others, you reflect the greatness God designed for you. So rise with purpose. Serve with joy. Seek Him with all your heart. The greatness in you is not just potential—it's a divine calling waiting to be lived.

Set Apart for Significance

1. Humble

Humility is the foundation of true greatness. It begins with recognizing that everything we have—our talents, opportunities, and even breath—is a gift from God. A humble person does not seek applause but seeks to please the One who gave them life. Jesus modeled humility by washing His disciples' feet, showing that leadership begins with service. When we humble ourselves, we open the door for God to lift us up in His perfect timing. Scripture says, *"Humble yourselves before the Lord, and He will lift you up"* (**James 4:10**). Greatness is not found in pride, but in surrender. A humble heart is teachable, gentle, and full of grace. It listens more than it speaks and values others above self. Moses was called the most humble man on earth, and God used him to lead a nation. Humility allows us to walk in wisdom, avoid destruction, and reflect the character of Christ. Without humility, greatness becomes hollow and self-serving.

Humility also creates space for growth. When we admit we don't know everything, we become open to learning and transformation. A proud heart resists correction, but a humble spirit welcomes it. Great leaders are often those who have failed, learned, and risen again with grace. They don't pretend to be perfect—they acknowledge their weaknesses and rely on God's strength. Humility builds strong relationships because it removes the need to compete or compare. It allows us to celebrate others without feeling threatened. Jesus said, *"Whoever wants to become great among you must be your servant"* (**Matthew 20:26**). That means greatness is not about being first—it's about putting others first. When we live humbly, we become approachable, trustworthy, and wise. We stop chasing status and start pursuing purpose. In God's kingdom, the lowly are lifted up, and the meek inherit the earth.

2. Help

Helping others is one of the clearest signs of greatness. It shows that your heart is aligned with God's command to love your neighbor. When you help someone in need, you become a vessel of hope and healing. Jesus said, *"It is more blessed to give than to receive"* (**Acts 20:35**), reminding us that greatness is found in generosity. Helping doesn't require wealth—it requires willingness. The Good Samaritan helped a wounded stranger, proving that compassion is more powerful than status. Great people look for opportunities to lift others up, even when it's inconvenient. They don't wait to be asked—they act out of love. Helping builds trust, strengthens communities, and reflects God's heart. It's not about being seen—it's about making a difference. When you help others, you grow in empathy, wisdom, and influence. Greatness is measured by how many lives you touch, not how many trophies you collect.

Helping also transforms the helper. When you give your time, energy, or resources to someone else, you become more aware of your own blessings. It shifts your focus from self to service. Helping others teaches patience, compassion, and humility. It reminds us that we are all connected and that no act of kindness is ever wasted. Jesus healed, fed, and comforted people—not for recognition, but because He loved deeply. When we follow His example, we step into our divine calling. Helping others can be as simple as listening, encouraging, or praying. It doesn't require a platform—just a willing heart. Scripture says, *"Carry each other's burdens, and in this way you will fulfill the law of Christ"* (**Galatians 6:2**). That means helping is not optional—it's essential. When we help, we reflect the love of God and become agents of change.

3. Honor

Honor is the act of showing respect, value, and dignity to others. It's a powerful trait that reflects the heart of God, who honors those who walk in righteousness. To honor someone is to recognize their worth, even when the world overlooks them. Scripture says, *"Honor one another above yourselves"* (**Romans 12:10**), reminding us that greatness is rooted in humility and respect. David honored King Saul, even when Saul tried to kill him, showing restraint and reverence for God's anointed. Honor builds bridges, not walls—it creates trust and unity. Great people honor their parents, leaders, and even their enemies. They speak with kindness, act with integrity, and treat others with dignity. Honor is not weakness—it's strength under control. It elevates relationships and invites God's favor. When you live with honor, you reflect the character of Christ and inspire others to do the same. Greatness without honor is empty; greatness with honor is eternal.

Honor also means living with integrity. It's not just about how you treat others—it's about how you carry yourself. A person of honor keeps their word, stands for truth, and lives with consistency. They don't compromise their values for popularity or gain. Honor means doing the right thing, even when no one is watching. It's about being trustworthy, dependable, and faithful. Jesus honored His Father in everything He did, and His life was marked by obedience and reverence. When we honor God, we align ourselves with His will. Scripture says, *"Those who honor Me I will honor"* (**1 Samuel 2:30**). That means honor brings reward—not just from people, but from God Himself. Living with honor sets you apart and builds a legacy that lasts. It's a quiet strength that speaks louder than words. Greatness begins when honor becomes your lifestyle.

4. Handle

To handle life well is to face challenges with wisdom, grace, and strength. Greatness is not found in avoiding problems but in how you respond to them. When you handle pressure calmly, you show maturity and leadership. Joseph was betrayed, sold into slavery, and imprisoned, yet he handled each season with faith and integrity. His ability to manage adversity prepared him for greatness in Egypt. Scripture says, *"A gentle answer turns away wrath, but a harsh* word *stirs up anger*" (**Proverbs 15:1**). Handling conflict with gentleness can defuse tension and build trust. Great people don't panic—they pray and plan. They don't react impulsively—they respond with clarity and purpose. Handling responsibility well earns respect and opens doors. Whether it's managing emotions, relationships, or decisions, how you handle life reveals your character. Greatness grows in the soil of calm, wise handling of life's storms.

Handling also means being dependable under pressure. It's about showing up when it's hard and staying steady when others fall apart. Leaders who handle stress with grace become anchors for their teams and families. They don't let fear dictate their actions—they lean on faith. Jesus handled betrayal, rejection, and suffering with unwavering love and purpose. His example teaches us that greatness is not about control—it's about surrender and strength. When you handle criticism with humility, you grow. When you handle success with gratitude, you stay grounded. Handling life well means knowing when to speak and when to stay silent. It means being thoughtful, not reactive. Scripture reminds us, *"The wise store up knowledge, but the mouth of a fool invites ruin"* (**Proverbs 10:14**). Greatness is revealed in how you carry yourself through both triumph and trial.

5. Heal

Healing is one of the most powerful expressions of greatness. It's not limited to physical recovery—it includes emotional, spiritual, and relational restoration. Jesus healed the sick, comforted the brokenhearted, and forgave sins, showing that healing is central to His mission. Scripture says, *"He heals the brokenhearted and binds up their wounds"* (**Psalm 147:3**). Great people bring healing through their words, actions, and presence. They listen deeply, speak gently, and love fiercely. Healing others requires empathy, patience, and spiritual strength. It's not about fixing—it's about restoring what was lost. When you help someone heal from pain, rejection, or fear, you reflect the love of Christ. Healing creates freedom, joy, and transformation. It's a gift that multiplies—when you heal others, you often find healing yourself.

Healing also requires courage. It means facing wounds instead of hiding them. Greatness is found in those who are willing to walk with others through their darkest valleys. You don't need to have all the answers—you just need to be present and compassionate. Jesus didn't rush people through their pain—He met them in it. When you offer forgiveness, encouragement, or comfort, you become a healer. Healing builds bridges and breaks chains. It restores dignity and renews hope. Scripture says, *"Therefore encourage one another and build each other up"* (**1 Thessalonians 5:11**). That's what healing does—it builds people up from the inside out. Greatness is not just about power—it's about the ability to restore what's broken. When you choose to heal instead of hurt, you become a light in someone's darkness.

6. Harmonize

To harmonize is to bring unity, peace, and cooperation among people. Greatness is not loud—it's often quiet, working behind the scenes to create connection. Nehemiah harmonized the people of Jerusalem to rebuild the city walls, overcoming opposition through unity. Scripture says, *"If it is possible, as far as it depends on you, live at peace with everyone"* (**Romans 12:18**). Harmonizing requires humility, patience, and wisdom. It means choosing peace over pride and unity over division. Great people don't stir conflict—they resolve it. They listen to understand, not just to reply. Harmonizing creates strength in families, teams, and communities. It's the glue that holds relationships together. When you harmonize, you reflect the heart of God, who desires unity among His children. Greatness thrives in environments of peace and purpose.

Harmony also means valuing differences. It's not about making everyone the same—it's about blending strengths for a greater good. Great leaders know how to bring people together without erasing their uniqueness. They create space for collaboration, not competition. Jesus prayed that His followers would be one, just as He and the Father are one (**John 17:21).** That kind of unity is powerful and transformative. Harmonizing requires emotional intelligence and spiritual maturity. It means being a peacemaker, not a peacekeeper. Peacemakers actively build bridges and resolve tension. Scripture says, *"Blessed are the peacemakers, for they will be called children of God"* (**Matthew 5:9**). When you harmonize, you create environments where greatness can grow. Unity doesn't just feel good—it multiplies impact and influence.

7. Hope in the Lord

Hope in God is the anchor of true greatness. It keeps you steady when life is uncertain and fuels your faith when the road is long. Abraham hoped against hope and believed God's promise, becoming the father of nations. Scripture says, *"Those who hope in the Lord will renew their strength"* (**Isaiah 40:31**). Hope is not wishful thinking—it's confident trust in God's character. Great people don't give up—they look up. They believe in what they cannot see because they trust the One who sees all. Hope gives you endurance, courage, and vision. It lifts your eyes above the storm and reminds you that God is faithful. When you hope in the Lord, you walk with confidence, not fear. You inspire others to believe, dream, and persevere. Greatness is not just about what you achieve—it's about who you trust.

SYAVIHA MULENGYA

Hope also fuels resilience. It allows you to keep going when others quit. When your hope is in God, setbacks become setups for something greater. David hoped in God even when he was hunted and heartbroken. His psalms are filled with cries of pain and declarations of trust. Hope doesn't deny reality—it declares that God is greater than it. Scripture says, *"May the God of hope fill you with all joy and peace as you trust in Him"* (**Romans 15:13**). That kind of hope transforms your mindset and your future. It gives you strength to rise, even when you've been knocked down. Greatness is sustained by hope that refuses to die. When you hope in the Lord, you become a beacon of light in a world that often feels dark. Your hope becomes contagious, and your life becomes a testimony of God's faithfulness.

Called for Greatness

True greatness, according to Scripture, is not measured by status, wealth, or applause—it is revealed through character, obedience, and love. It begins with humility, the quiet strength that bows before God and lifts others without seeking recognition. Greatness is found in servanthood, where the heart chooses to serve rather than be served, just as Jesus did. It is expressed through love and compassion, shown in acts of kindness, forgiveness, and sacrificial care. Obedience to God, even when the path is difficult, marks the lives of those like Abraham and Moses, who trusted God above all. Transformation is another sign—when a life turns from brokenness to purpose, as Paul did, it reflects divine greatness. Wisdom and integrity guide great individuals to make decisions rooted in truth, like David, who pursued God's heart despite his failures. Faith in action is the final thread, trusting God boldly even when the outcome is unseen. These traits do not shout—they whisper strength, courage, and grace. Greatness is not about being noticed—it's about being faithful. You are called to this kind of greatness: to live with purpose, serve with love, and walk humbly with your God.

Actions That Speak Louder Than Pride

1. Listening

Humility is reflected in the way we listen to others. A humble person listens without interrupting or dismissing others' words. They take the time to truly hear and understand different opinions, showing respect for others' thoughts and feelings. This kind of listening creates an open and supportive environment where people feel valued and heard. Listening with humility means putting aside our own need to be right and choosing to be present. It's about giving others space to speak and honoring their voice. When we listen well, we build trust and show that we care. Humble listening is patient, gentle, and full of grace. It doesn't rush to respond—it waits to understand. As **James 1:19** teaches, *"Everyone should be quick to listen, slow to speak and slow to become angry."* This verse reminds us that listening is a spiritual discipline that reflects humility. Through listening, we connect deeply and build stronger relationships.

Listening with humility goes beyond just hearing words—it involves seeking to understand the heart behind them. A humble listener doesn't judge or assume; they ask questions and show genuine interest. They recognize that every person has a story worth hearing. This kind of listening fosters peace and unity. It helps resolve disagreements without conflict and builds bridges where pride would build walls. Humility through listening creates a safe space for honesty and healing. It shows others that they matter and that their voice is important. When we listen with humility, we learn more about others and ourselves. We grow in empathy and compassion. We become better friends, leaders, and family members. Listening is one of the simplest yet most powerful ways to show humility. And in doing so, we reflect the love and patience of Christ.

2. Learning

Humility involves a deep willingness to learn. A humble person knows they don't have all the answers and is open to gaining new knowledge. They are teachable, curious, and eager to grow. Humility helps us admit when we're wrong and seek wisdom to do better. It keeps us from becoming arrogant or closed-minded. A humble learner asks questions, listens to advice, and welcomes correction. They understand that learning is a lifelong journey. As **Proverbs 9:9** says, *"Instruct the wise and they will be wiser still; teach the righteous and they will add to their learning."* This verse shows that wisdom grows when we stay humble. Learning keeps us grounded and helps us improve continuously. It allows us to grow in character, not just in knowledge. Humility makes learning a joy, not a burden.

A humble person doesn't pretend to know everything—they embrace the opportunity to learn from others. They see every experience as a chance to grow. Whether through books, conversations, or challenges, they remain open and teachable. Humility helps us learn from failure without shame and from success without pride. It teaches us to value the wisdom of others and to seek truth with sincerity. Humble learners are not afraid to say, "I don't know," because they trust that growth comes through honesty. They are not defensive—they are reflective. They welcome feedback and use it to become better. Humility in learning leads to wisdom, maturity, and deeper understanding. It helps us become more thoughtful, more compassionate, and more effective in everything we do. When we learn with humility, we grow in grace. And that growth blesses everyone around us.

3. Looking After Others

Humility is shown through genuine care for others. A humble person looks beyond their own needs and extends a helping hand to those around them. They are not self-centered—they are others-focused. Humility teaches us to see people through the eyes of compassion. It helps us notice when someone is hurting and respond with kindness. A humble heart doesn't wait to be asked—it offers help freely. This selfless attitude uplifts those who receive care and strengthens community bonds. As **Philippians 2:4** reminds us, *"Not looking to your own interests but each of you to the interests of the others."* This verse calls us to live with empathy and generosity. Humility creates an environment of love and support. It makes people feel seen, valued, and cared for. Looking after others is one of the clearest signs of a humble spirit.

Caring for others with humility means putting their well-being first. It's not about gaining recognition—it's about making a difference. Humble people serve quietly, without expecting anything in return. They offer their time, energy, and resources to meet the needs of others. They celebrate others' victories and walk with them through struggles. Humility helps us be present, patient, and kind. It teaches us to love without limits and to give without conditions. When we care for others humbly, we build trust and deepen relationships. We create a culture of compassion and unity. Humility reminds us that we are all connected and that every act of kindness matters. Looking after others is not just a duty—it's a privilege. And through it, we reflect the heart of Christ.

SYAVIHA MULENGYA

4. Loving

Humility is expressed through love that is patient, kind, and unconditional. A humble person doesn't love to be noticed—they love to make others feel seen. Their love is not boastful or proud, but gentle and sincere. They show care through small acts of kindness, thoughtful words, and a willingness to serve. Humility allows us to love without expecting anything in return. It helps us forgive easily, speak gently, and give generously. Love rooted in humility is steady and strong—it doesn't fade when things get hard. As **1 Corinthians 13:4-5** reminds us, *"Love is patient, love is kind. It does not envy, it does not boast, it is not proud."* This kind of love builds trust and brings healing. It creates safe spaces where people feel valued and accepted. Humble love doesn't seek attention—it seeks connection. And in that connection, lives are changed.

Loving with humility means putting others first and choosing compassion over criticism. It means seeing the best in people, even when they're struggling. A humble person loves without judgment and supports without conditions. They don't keep score—they keep showing up. Their love is consistent, even when it's not convenient. Humility helps us love with grace, not ego. It teaches us to be patient with others' flaws and gentle with their hearts. Loving humbly means listening, serving, and encouraging. It's not about being perfect—it's about being present. Humble love builds bridges, not walls. It brings peace into conflict and hope into despair. And through this kind of love, we reflect the heart of God.

5. Leading

Humility in leadership means serving others with integrity and compassion. A humble leader doesn't seek power—they seek purpose. They lead by example, not by force. Their strength comes from their willingness to listen, support, and guide. Humble leaders build others up and celebrate their success. They don't need to be the loudest—they choose to be the most caring. As **Matthew 20:26-28** teaches, *"Whoever wants to become great among you must be your servant."* Jesus modeled servant leadership, showing that true greatness comes through humility. A humble leader creates a safe and positive environment where everyone can thrive. They value each person's contribution and make space for growth. Their leadership is marked by kindness, wisdom, and grace. And in that grace, teams flourish.

Leading with humility means putting the needs of others before personal gain. It means being approachable, teachable, and honest. A humble leader admits mistakes and learns from them. They don't pretend to know everything—they invite collaboration. Their leadership is not about control—it's about connection. Humility helps leaders build trust and inspire loyalty. It creates a culture of respect and unity. Humble leaders empower others to lead and grow. They don't seek credit—they share it. Their influence comes from their character, not their title. Leading humbly transforms workplaces, families, and communities. And through it, we reflect the servant heart of Christ.

6. Letting Go

Humility teaches us the power of letting go—especially of grudges, pride, and past hurts. A humble person understands that forgiveness is not weakness—it's wisdom. They choose peace over bitterness and healing over resentment. Letting go means releasing the need to be right and embracing the need to be free. It's about moving forward with grace, not staying stuck in anger. Humility helps us forgive others, even when it's hard. As **Colossians 3:13** reminds us, "Bear with each other and forgive one another... Forgive as the Lord forgave you." This kind of forgiveness brings

SYAVIHA MULENGYA

peace to our hearts and healing to our relationships. It allows us to grow instead of remaining wounded. Humble people don't hold mistakes over others—they offer mercy. They understand that everyone needs grace. And in giving it, they find freedom.

Letting go through humility also means releasing control and trusting God. It means surrendering our plans, our pride, and our pain. A humble heart doesn't cling to what hurts—it opens to what heals. Forgiveness is a gift we give ourselves and others. It creates space for reconciliation and renewal. Humble people don't dwell on the past—they learn from it and move forward. They choose understanding over judgment and compassion over revenge. Letting go is not forgetting—it's choosing peace. It's saying, "I won't let this define me—I'll let it refine me." Humility helps us let go with love, not bitterness. And in that release, we find strength, clarity, and joy.

7. Lending a Hand

Humility is clearly seen in the act of helping others. A humble person doesn't wait to be asked—they step in with kindness and care. They offer their time, energy, and resources without expecting anything in return. Helping others is not a duty—it's a joy. Humility teaches us to carry each other's burdens with love. As **Galatians 6:2** says, *"Carry each other's burdens, and in this way you will fulfill the law of Christ."* This kind of support creates strong, compassionate communities. It builds trust and deepens relationships. Humble people help quietly, but their impact is loud. They don't seek praise—they seek to make a difference. Lending a hand is one of the most powerful ways to show humility. And through it, we reflect the heart of Jesus.

Helping others with humility also fosters unity and a sense of belonging. A humble person values everyone and works to include

SYAVIHA MULENGYA

them. They remove barriers and build bridges. They encourage dialogue and foster peace. As **Ephesians 4:3** reminds us, *"Make every effort to keep the unity of the Spirit through the bond of pcacc."* Humility helps us see others as equals, not competitors. It teaches us to serve with joy and love with intention. Lending a hand brings people together and strengthens community bonds. It creates a culture of kindness where everyone feels safe and supported. Humble helpers don't just fix problems—they build people. And in doing so, they create a world filled with grace, generosity, and hope.

4

---·~·---

Success Is A Gift, Handle It With Humility.

S uccess is a blessing from God, not something we achieve by our strength alone. It is a gift that should be received with gratitude, not pride. When we succeed, we must remember who gave us the ability to do so. **Deuteronomy 8:18** says, *"Remember the Lord your God, for it is He who gives you the ability to produce wealth."* This verse reminds us that every achievement is a result of God's grace. A humble heart gives thanks and does not boast. It uses success to serve others, not to elevate self. True humility keeps us grounded, even when we rise. It helps us stay focused on purpose, not popularity. When we honor God with our success, we bring glory to His name. We must never forget that success is temporary, but character lasts forever. Let your victories reflect God's goodness, not your own greatness.

Handling success with humility means staying teachable and kind. It means lifting others up instead of looking down on them. A humble person celebrates quietly and leads gently. They know that success is not a destination—it's a responsibility. **Proverbs 3:34** says,

"He mocks proud mockers but shows favor to the humble and oppressed." God blesses those who walk in humility. When we succeed, we should ask, "How can I use this to help others?" Humility turns success into service. It transforms achievement into impact. It reminds us that we are stewards, not owners. Let your success be a light, not a spotlight. And through it all, keep your heart soft, your spirit thankful, and your eyes on God.

Let your character shine brighter than your accomplishments

1. Count It as a Blessing

Success is not something we earn alone—it's a gift from God. When we achieve something, we should first pause and thank Him for the opportunity, the strength, and the favor. **James 1:17** says, *"Every good and perfect gift is from above."* Recognizing success as a blessing keeps us humble and grateful. It reminds us that we are not self-made but God-supported. Gratitude protects us from pride and helps us stay grounded. When we count our blessings, we also become more generous and joyful. Success should lead us to worship, not boast. It's a moment to reflect on God's goodness. A thankful heart honors the source of the blessing. And when we give thanks, we open the door for even greater things.

Counting success as a blessing also helps us see it as a responsibility. Blessings are meant to be shared, not hoarded. When we view success through the lens of stewardship, we begin to ask, "How can I use this to help others?" This mindset shifts our focus from self to service. It keeps us from becoming arrogant or entitled. Success becomes a tool for impact, not just a personal achievement. A humble heart sees every win as a chance to glorify God. It's not about taking credit—it's about giving thanks. When we count success as a blessing, we stay rooted in grace. We remember that every step forward is guided by His hand. And that truth keeps us walking in humility and purpose.

2. Connect with God and People

Success should never isolate us—it should draw us closer to God and others. When we succeed, it's easy to get caught up in the moment and forget our need for connection. But **John 15:5** reminds us, *"Apart from Me you can do nothing."* Staying connected to God keeps our hearts aligned with His will. It helps us stay humble, focused, and spiritually strong. Prayer and worship should increase, not decrease, in seasons of success. We also need people— mentors, friends, and loved ones—to keep us balanced. They offer wisdom, support, and accountability. Success is sweeter when shared with others. Connection builds community and keeps pride in check. It reminds us that we're part of something bigger than ourselves.

Connecting with others also means being present and approachable. Don't let success make you distant or unrelatable. Stay kind, listen well, and be available. People need to see that your heart hasn't changed, even if your circumstances have. Humility keeps relationships strong. It allows you to celebrate with others and support them in their own journeys. When you stay connected, you build trust and deepen bonds. Success should never be a wall— it should be a bridge. Let it bring you closer to God through gratitude and prayer. Let It bring you closer to people through love and service. In connection, success becomes a blessing that multiplies.

3. Conquer Pride

Pride is one of the greatest dangers that comes with success. It whispers, "You did this all by yourself," and tempts us to forget

SYAVIHA MULENGYA

God's role. But **Proverbs 16:18** warns, *"Pride goes before destruction, a haughty spirit before a fall."* To handle success well, we must daily conquer pride. That means staying humble, giving credit where it's due, and remembering our dependence on God. Pride isolates, but humility connects. It's not weakness—it's wisdom. A humble heart is teachable, kind, and full of grace. Conquering pride helps us stay balanced and focused. It keeps our character strong and our relationships healthy. When we defeat pride, we protect the blessing.

Conquering pride also means being honest about our limitations. No one is perfect, and success doesn't make us immune to mistakes. A humble person admits when they're wrong and learns from it. They don't pretend to have all the answers—they seek wisdom. Pride resists correction, but humility embraces growth. When we conquer pride, we open the door to deeper wisdom and lasting impact. We become better leaders, friends, and followers of Christ. Success handled with humility becomes a testimony, not a trap. It reflects God's goodness, not our greatness. And in that reflection, others are inspired and encouraged.

4. Count on God

Success can be overwhelming, and it's easy to rely on our own strength. But true peace and direction come from counting on God. **Psalm 20:7** says, *"Some trust in chariots and some in horses, but we trust in the name of the Lord our God."* When we lean on Him, we find wisdom, clarity, and strength. Counting on God means praying before making decisions. It means seeking His will above our own. It's trusting that He knows what's best, even when we don't understand. Success is not a reason to stop depending on God—it's a reason to depend on Him more. He is our source, our guide, and our protector.

SYAVIHA MULENGYA

Counting on God also means surrendering control. We may have plans, but God's purpose will always prevail. A humble heart says, "Lord, lead me." It doesn't rush ahead—it waits on His timing. When we count on God, we walk in peace, not pressure. We stop striving and start trusting. Success becomes a journey of faith, not just achievement. It's not about being strong—it's about being surrendered. God's strength is made perfect in our weakness. And when we rely on Him, we handle success with grace and wisdom.

5. Contribute

Success is not just for personal gain—it's an opportunity to give back. When we contribute to others, we turn our blessings into blessings for someone else. A humble person sees success as a tool to serve, not a trophy to display. **1 Peter 4:10** says, *"Each of you should use whatever gift you have received to serve others."* This reminds us that our talents and achievements are meant to help others grow. Contributing builds community and spreads hope. It shows that we care more about impact than image. When we give generously, we reflect the heart of God. Success becomes meaningful when it's shared. Whether it's time, wisdom, or resources, giving completes success. A giving spirit keeps pride away and invites joy in.

Contributing also helps us stay connected to our purpose. It reminds us that we are part of something bigger than ourselves. When we help others, we grow in compassion and humility. Success should never make us selfish—it should make us more selfless. Giving is not about losing—it's about multiplying blessings. A generous heart is a humble heart. When we contribute, we build trust and strengthen relationships. We become a light in someone else's darkness. God honors those who give with joy and sincerity. **Acts 20:35** says, *"It is more blessed to give than to receive."* That truth transforms how we view success. It's not about what we have—it's about what we give.

6. Continue

Success is not the finish line—it's a step forward. When we succeed, we must keep growing, learning, and improving. A humble person doesn't settle—they continue to pursue excellence. **Philippians 3:14** says, *"I press on toward the goal to win the prize for which God has called me."* This verse reminds us to keep moving forward with purpose. Success should never make us lazy or proud. It should inspire us to do more, serve more, and grow more. Continuing means staying faithful to your calling. It means not letting comfort stop your progress. A humble heart keeps striving with grace. It knows that growth is a journey, not a destination. And every step forward is a chance to honor God.

Continuing also means staying committed to your values. Success can tempt us to compromise, but humility keeps us anchored. A person who continues with integrity builds a legacy that lasts. They don't chase fame—they chase faithfulness. When we keep going, we inspire others to do the same. We show that success is not about one moment—it's about a lifetime of purpose. A humble person keeps learning, even when they're praised. They stay open to feedback and hungry for wisdom. **Proverbs 4:7** says, *"The beginning of wisdom is this: Get wisdom. Though it cost all you have, get understanding."* Continuing with humility leads to deeper insight and greater impact. It keeps our hearts soft and our mission clear.

7. Consult

Success should never make us think we know it all. A humble person seeks advice, wisdom, and guidance. They consult God first,

SYAVIHA MULENGYA

and then trust people around them. **Proverbs 15:22** says, *"Plans fail for lack of counsel, but with many advisers they succeed."* This shows that wise counsel leads to lasting success. Consulting others helps us avoid mistakes and grow in understanding. It keeps us teachable and open-minded. A humble heart asks questions and listens well. It values wisdom over ego. When we consult others, we build stronger decisions. We show that we respect their insight and experience. And in doing so, we grow wiser ourselves.

Consulting God is even more important. Prayer should be our first step, not our last resort. **James 1:5** says, *"If any of you lacks wisdom, you should ask God, who gives generously to all."* God's guidance is perfect and full of grace. When we seek Him, we find clarity and peace. Success handled with prayer becomes a testimony of faith. It shows that we trust God more than our own plans. A humble person consults God daily, asking for direction and strength. They don't rush—they wait on His timing. Consulting keeps us aligned with His will. It helps us walk in wisdom, not pride. And that kind of success brings lasting joy.

8. Celebrate

Celebrating success is important—but it should be done with humility. A humble person rejoices without boasting. They give thanks to God and honor those who helped along the way. **Psalm 126:3** says, *"The Lord has done great things for us, and we are filled with joy."* Celebration is a way to express gratitude, not pride. It reminds us of how far we've come and who brought us there. A humble celebration includes others and lifts them up. It's not about showing off—it's about sharing joy. When we celebrate with grace, we build unity and encouragement. We inspire others to keep going. Success becomes a shared victory, not a solo moment. And in that joy, we reflect God's goodness.

SYAVIHA MULENGYA

Celebrating also helps us pause and reflect. It's easy to rush to the next goal, but humility teaches us to be present. A humble heart celebrates with thankfulness and peace. It doesn't exaggerate—it appreciates. Celebration is a chance to honor God publicly. It's a moment to say, "Thank You, Lord, for all You've done." When we celebrate well, we stay grounded. We remember that every win is a gift, not a guarantee. **1 Thessalonians 5:18** says, *"Give thanks in all circumstances."* That includes moments of success. A humble celebration brings joy to others and glory to God. And it prepares our hearts for the next step in the journey

9. Check and Correct

Success should never make us blind to our weaknesses. A humble person regularly checks their heart, motives, and actions. They ask, "Am I still walking in truth? Am I honoring God with this success?" **Lamentations 3:40** says, *"Let us examine our ways and test them, and let us return to the Lord."* This verse reminds us to reflect and realign. Checking ourselves helps us stay on the right path. It prevents pride from creeping in and keeps our spirit pure. When we pause to evaluate, we grow in wisdom. We become more aware of areas that need change. Success is not just about doing well—it's about doing right. A humble heart is always willing to improve.

Correcting ourselves means making adjustments when we see something off. It's not about guilt—it's about growth. A wise person doesn't ignore mistakes—they learn from them. **Proverbs 12:1** says, *"Whoever loves discipline loves knowledge, but whoever hates correction is stupid."* God honors those who are willing to change. Correction leads to maturity and a deeper impact. It helps us stay faithful and focused. When we correct our course, we protect our character. We show that success hasn't made us stubborn—it's made us stronger. A humble person welcomes correction as a gift. They know that growth requires honesty. And through that honesty, they become even more effective and trustworthy.

10. Choose Wisely

Success opens many doors—but not every door is meant to be walked through. A humble person chooses wisely, guided by values and vision. They don't chase every opportunity—they seek God's direction. **Proverbs 3:6** says, *"In all your ways submit to Him, and He will make your paths straight."* Wise choices protect us from distractions and regrets. They help us stay aligned with our purpose. Success can be loud, but wisdom is quiet and clear. Choosing wisely means saying "no" to things that don't fit your calling. It means prioritizing what matters most. A humble heart doesn't rush—it reflects. It asks, "Is this God's best for me?" And it listens for His answer.

Wise choices also shape your legacy. What you choose today will echo into tomorrow. A humble person thinks long-term, not just short-term. They choose integrity over popularity, and purpose over pressure. **Psalm 25:12** says, *"Who, then, are those who fear the Lord? He will instruct them in the ways they should choose."* God promises to guide those who seek Him. Choosing wisely means surrounding yourself with godly counsel. It means staying true to your values, even when it's hard. Success handled with wisdom becomes a blessing that lasts. It brings peace, clarity, and impact. And in every choice, we reflect the heart of God.

Stay Wise in Your Winning Season

1. Submit Before God

God gives us success so we can learn to submit to Him with a thankful heart. Success is not just a reward—it's a reminder that we need His guidance. When we succeed, we must bow before Him and say, "Lord, this is Yours." **Proverbs 3:6** says, *"In all your ways submit to Him, and He will make your paths straight."* Submission keeps us humble and focused on God's purpose. It helps us avoid pride and walk in obedience. Success without submission leads to confusion and pride. But when we submit, we find peace and direction. God wants our hearts to stay soft, even when we rise. He gives success to those who will honor Him with it. True success begins with surrender.

2. Strengthen Others

God gives us success so we can lift others up. It's not just about personal gain—it's about helping people grow. **Romans 15:2** says, *"Each of us should please our neighbors for their good, to build them up."* When we succeed, we have the chance to encourage and support others. Our story can give someone else hope. Strength is not for showing off—it's for sharing. God blesses us so we can be a blessing. Success becomes meaningful when it helps others rise. A strong person helps others become stronger. God's plan is always bigger than one person. Success is a tool to build others, not just ourselves.

3. Serve God and Others

Success is a chance to serve, not to be served. God gives us influence so we can use it for good. **Galatians 5:13** says, *"Serve one another humbly in love."* Serving shows that we care more about impact than image. When we succeed, we must ask, "How can I use this to help?" God loves a servant heart. True greatness comes from serving with joy. Success should lead us to action, not comfort. Serving others reflects the love of Christ. God gives success to those who will use it for His glory. A servant heart makes success shine brighter.

SYAVIHA MULENGYA

4. Solve Problems

God gives us success to bring solutions to the world. He wants us to be problem-solvers, not just dreamers. **Proverbs 2:6-7** says, *"For the Lord gives wisdom... He holds success in store for the upright."* Success gives us the tools to fix what's broken. It helps us bring healing, ideas, and answers. God uses our gifts to meet real needs. When we solve problems, we reflect His wisdom. We become part of His plan to restore and renew. Success is not just about achievement—it's about impact. God gives success to those who will use it to make things better. Solving problems is part of our calling.

5. Shine for His Glory

Success is meant to shine—but not for our fame. God gives us success so we can reflect His light. **Matthew 5:16** says, *"Let your light shine before others... and glorify your Father in heaven."* When we succeed, people should see God's goodness in us. Our lives become a testimony of His grace. Shining means living with joy, kindness, and purpose. It's not about being noticed—it's about making God known. Every achievement is a chance to point to Him. God wants our success to lead others to Him. When we shine for His glory, we fulfill our true purpose. Success becomes worship when it reflects His light.

6. Show the Way and Set a Good Example

God gives us success so we can lead by example. People are watching how we live, especially when we succeed. **1 Timothy 4:12** says, *"Set an example for the believers in speech, in conduct, in love, in faith and in purity."* A good example inspires others to follow the right path. Success should never make us proud—it should make us responsible. When we live with integrity, we guide others well. God wants us to be lights in a dark world. Our choices speak louder than our words. Success gives us influence, and influence must be used wisely. A godly example can change lives. God gives success to those who will lead with love.

7. Support

God gives us success so we can support others in their journey. Life is not meant to be lived alone. **Ecclesiastes 4:9-10** says, *"Two are better than one... if either of them falls, one can help the other up."* Success gives us the strength to lift others when they're weak. It allows us to be a shoulder, a helper, and a friend. God wants us to use our blessings to bless others. Supporting others builds unity and love. It shows that we care more about people than position. Success becomes powerful when it's shared. God gives success to those who will carry others with them. Support is a gift we give from the overflow of grace.

Don't Let Success Ruin You

1. Leave God Behind

Success should never lead us away from God—it should draw us closer. When we forget the One who gave us the victory, we risk losing the very foundation that brought us there. **Deuteronomy 8:18** says, *"Remember the Lord your God, for it is He who gives you the ability to produce wealth."* Leaving God behind means walking in pride, not purpose. It's easy to get caught up in achievements and forget the source of our strength. But true success is sustained only when we stay connected to Him. God wants to be part of every step, not just the beginning. When we honor Him in success, He continues to guide us. Leaving God behind leads to emptiness, even when everything looks full. Stay close to Him, and your success will have eternal value.

2. Live Carelessly

Success is not a license to live without discipline. When we live carelessly, we waste the opportunities God has given us. **Ephesians 5:15** says, *"Be very careful, then, how you live—not as unwise but as wise."* Carelessness leads to poor choices, broken relationships, and missed blessings. Success should make us more thoughtful, not reckless. We are called to live with purpose, even in prosperity. Every decision matters, and every moment counts. Living wisely honors God and protects our future. Carelessness can destroy what took years to build. Success is a gift—don't treat it lightly. Live with intention, and your life will shine with meaning.

3. Laugh at Others

Mocking others in their struggle is never part of God's plan. Success should make us more compassionate, not more critical. **Proverbs 17:5** says, *"Whoever mocks the poor shows contempt for their Maker."* Laughing at others reveals pride, not strength. We are called to lift people up, not tear them down. Everyone is on a journey, and we don't know the battles they face. True success includes kindness and empathy. When we laugh at others, we forget that we were once in need, too. God blesses us so we can be a blessing. Let your words heal, not hurt. Choose grace over mockery, and your success will inspire others.

4. Look Down on Others

Success should never make us feel superior. Looking down on others creates division and pride. **Romans 12:16** says, *"Do not be proud, but be willing to associate with people of low position."* Every person matters to God, no matter their status. When we look down, we miss the beauty in others. Humility keeps us grounded and open-hearted. God lifts up those who lift others. True greatness is found in serving, not in judging. Success is not a pedestal—it's a platform to love. Treat everyone with respect, and your influence will grow. Looking down limits your vision—lift others up instead.

5. Lose Focus

Success can be distracting if we're not careful. It's easy to chase applause and forget our purpose. **Proverbs 4:25** says, *"Let your eyes look straight ahead; fix your gaze directly before you."* Losing focus leads to wasted time and missed opportunities. Stay centered on what matters most—your calling, your values, and your relationship with God. Don't let success pull you in every direction. Focus brings clarity, peace, and progress. When you stay focused, you build something that lasts. Distractions will come, but discipline keeps you steady. Success is not just about reaching goals—it's about staying true to your mission. Keep your eyes on the path God has set before you.

6. Lean on Your Own Strength

Success can tempt us to rely on ourselves instead of God. But our strength is limited—His is eternal. **Proverbs 3:5** says, *"Trust in the Lord with all your heart and lean not on your own understanding."* Leaning on your own strength leads to burnout and pride. God wants us to depend on Him, even when things are going well. He is our source, our guide, and our protector. When we lean on Him, we find peace and wisdom. Our talents are gifts, not guarantees. Success is safest in surrendered hands. Don't carry the weight alone—God is strong enough to hold it. Lean on Him, and your success will be secure.

7. Lie

Success should never come at the cost of truth. Lying to protect your image or gain more will only lead to loss. **Proverbs 12:22** says,

SYAVIHA MULENGYA

"The Lord detests lying lips, but He delights in people who are trustworthy." Truth builds trust, and trust builds legacy. Lies may bring short-term gain, but they destroy long-term peace. God honors honesty, even when it's hard. Success with integrity is far more valuable than success with secrets. Be honest in your words, your work, and your relationships. Let your success be clean and clear. Lies create confusion—truth brings freedom. Choose truth, and your life will shine with honor.

5

Pride Makes You
Miss The Best

Rise with gratitude, not pride.

Vuteke was a wealthy man whose pride and arrogance ruled his actions. One day, he visited a clinic in his community but refused to wait in line like everyone else. Believing his status as a rich man made him special, he demanded immediate attention. When the clinic staff politely explained the rules, Vuteke stormed out in anger, accusing the clinic of providing poor service. Using his influence, he pressured the local authorities to shut it down without any investigation. The closure left many families in the community struggling, as they were forced to travel long distances for medical care. Vuteke's pride made him blind to the impact his actions had on others, but fate would soon teach him a painful lesson.

One evening, Vuteke's young son suddenly fell ill, but neither he nor his wife was at home. The family worker, unable to drive Vuteke's luxurious cars, tried calling him repeatedly for help. Vuteke, thinking the calls were unimportant, ignored them and accused the worker of disturbing him. Desperate, the worker carried the child to the nearest clinic, only to discover that it had been shut down by Vuteke's orders. With no transportation and no other options, the child's condition worsened. When Vuteke finally returned home, he learned the devastating news that his son had passed away due to the lack of timely medical care. Overcome with grief, he blamed the worker, who responded sadly, "We tried to call you, but you rejected our calls." Vuteke's pride had not only cost the life of his son but also harmed his community. This tragic story serves as a powerful reminder of how pride blinds us to others' needs and leads to devastating consequences. Humility is the true path to greatness and peace.

The story of Vuteke shows us how pride can lead to painful consequences, not just for ourselves but also for those around us. Vuteke's success as a wealthy man made him believe he was above others, and his pride clouded his judgment. Instead of treating people with respect, he acted harshly, closing the clinic that was vital to the community simply because he didn't want to wait in line. Pride hardened him, refusing to listen to others or show compassion, even as his family worker repeatedly tried to reach him. It also made him heartless, as he ignored the calls for help, assuming they were unimportant. His pride turned what could have been a simple act of humility into a tragic loss for his son and the entire community. **Proverbs 16:18** warns us, *"Pride goes before destruction, a haughty spirit before a fall."* Vuteke's downfall is a reminder of this truth.

When success enters your life, it is important to remain grounded and humble. Pride can make you blind to the blessings God has given you and the people who support you. It can cause you to act without thinking, hurt those who rely on you, and create unnecessary conflict. Pride makes you see yourself as greater than others, leading to actions that harm relationships and create bitterness. **James 4:6** reminds us, *"God opposes the proud but shows favor to the humble."* Vuteke's story teaches us to value humility, which brings peace, wisdom, and meaningful connections. Humility allows us to recognize others' needs, act with kindness, and avoid the painful consequences of pride. Let Vuteke's story inspire you to choose humility and live a life that honors both God and the people around you.

Hurt people. Pride hurts the people around you by making you focus only on yourself. When you are full of pride, you forget to consider others' feelings and needs. This selfishness creates pain and disappointment for those who depend on you. Pride pushes people away, leaving loved ones feeling ignored or unimportant. The Bible encourages us in **Philippians 2:3,** *"Do nothing out of selfish ambition or vain conceit. Rather, in humility value others above yourselves."* Without humility, relationships are easily damaged, and the people you care about suffer unnecessarily.

1. Humiliate others.

Pride leads to humiliating others by putting them down to make yourself feel superior. Through harsh words or dismissive actions, pride can crush the confidence and dignity of others. This not only hurts their emotions but also creates resentment and division. Instead of lifting others up, pride focuses on tearing them down. **Proverbs 15:1** reminds us, *"A gentle answer turns away wrath, but a harsh word stirs up anger."* Humility, on the other hand, brings peace and uplifts others, while pride humiliates and causes harm.

2. Harm people

The story of Vuteke is a painful reminder of how pride can harm not only others but also yourself. Vuteke's wealth and status blinded him to the importance of treating others with kindness and fairness. His pride led him to shut down a community clinic simply because he refused to wait his turn in line, leaving many people without access to essential medical care. Tragically, when Vuteke's own son fell critically ill, the consequences of his arrogance became clear. His worker, unable to drive and desperate for help, tried calling Vuteke several times, but he ignored the calls, assuming they were unimportant. When the worker rushed the child to the nearest clinic, they found it closed—shut down by Vuteke's own actions. By the time Vuteke realized what had happened, it was too late, and his son had passed away. **Proverbs 16:18** warns, *"Pride goes before destruction, a haughty spirit before a fall."* Pride hardened Vuteke's heart, hurt the community, and ultimately brought unbearable grief to his family. His story teaches us that humility is the better path, allowing us to build loving relationships, act with compassion, and avoid the devastating consequences of pride.

3. Harden your heart

Pride hardens your heart, making it difficult for you to show love, forgive, or feel compassion. When your heart is hardened, you become cold and unapproachable, cutting yourself off from meaningful connections. This leads to bitterness and prevents healing. **Ezekiel 36:26** says, *"I will give you a new heart and put a new spirit in you; I will remove from you your heart of stone and give you a heart of flesh."* Choosing humility keeps your heart open, soft, and full of kindness.

4. Harass others

Pride often causes people to harass others by being overly demanding, critical, or controlling. When prideful, you try to assert dominance or superiority, which creates tension and fear in relationships. This behavior tears down trust and unity. **Colossians 4:6** tells us, *"Let your conversation be always full of grace, seasoned with salt."* Humility leads to grace and kindness, while pride creates unnecessary stress and conflict.

5. Hinder progress

Pride hinders your ability to grow and improve. When you are too proud to admit mistakes or listen to advice, you miss out on opportunities to learn and develop. Pride keeps you stuck in the same place, blocking personal and spiritual growth. **Proverbs 19:20** reminds us, *"Listen to advice and accept discipline, and at the end you will be counted among the wise."* Humility helps you move forward, while pride keeps you trapped.

6. Hurry decisions

Pride makes you rush into decisions without careful thought or consideration. You may act impulsively to protect your image or prove yourself, but this often leads to regret. **Proverbs 21:5** teaches, *"The plans of the diligent lead to profit as surely as haste leads to poverty."* A humble person takes their time to reflect and make wise choices, but pride causes haste and poor judgment

Is Pride Living in Me?

Pride doesn't always shout; it often whispers. It hides behind compliments, achievements, and even good intentions. It shows up when we think we're always right, when we resist correction, or when we quietly compare ourselves to others. Pride is subtle, but its effects are serious. **Proverbs 16:18** warns, *"Pride goes before destruction, a haughty spirit before a fall."* That means pride isn't just a bad attitude; it's a spiritual danger. It can block our prayers, damage relationships, and distance us from God. The question isn't whether pride exists in the world—it's whether it's quietly growing in our own hearts. We must ask, "Do I struggle to say sorry? Do I find it hard to celebrate others? Do I rely more on myself than on God?" These are signs that pride may be living in us.

1. Dominate

Pride often leads people to dominate others. It makes them feel they must be in control at all times. They may believe their way is the only right way. This attitude pushes others aside and silences their voices. It creates tension, not teamwork. Jesus taught that true greatness comes through serving others. **Matthew 20:26** says, *"Whoever wants to become great among you must be your servant."* Humility listens, shares, and includes. A dominating spirit breaks relationships and builds walls. God wants us to lead with love, not force. When we choose humility, we create space for others to grow. Take a moment to think about how you lead and treat those around you.

2. Demanding

Pride makes people demanding and self-focused. They expect others to meet their needs without question. This attitude can damage relationships and create resentment. Demanding people often ignore the feelings of others. They act as if they deserve special treatment. God teaches us to value others above ourselves. **Philippians 2:3** says, *"Do nothing out of selfish ambition or vain conceit."* Humility brings patience, kindness, and understanding. Being demanding shows a lack of compassion and maturity. True success includes caring for others, not just ourselves. A humble heart gives more than it asks. Think about how you respond when things don't go your way.

3. Defensive

Pride causes people to become defensive. They struggle to accept correction or feedback. A defensive person often reacts with anger or denial. This behavior blocks growth and learning. It keeps them from seeing their own faults. God wants us to be teachable and wise. **Proverbs 12:15** says, *"The wise listen to advice."* Humility helps us receive truth with grace. Defensiveness builds walls instead of bridges. A humble heart welcomes growth, even when it's hard. Listening well is a sign of strength, not weakness. Consider how you respond when someone offers you honest feedback.

4. Dictating

Pride leads to dictating behavior. A proud person may try to control every decision. They often ignore advice and input from others. This creates stress and weakens teamwork. Dictating shows a lack of trust and respect. God values collaboration and shared wisdom. **Proverbs 15:22** says, *"Plans fail for lack of counsel."* Humility invites others to speak and share. Dictating limits progress and causes division. Leading with humility builds unity and strength. A wise leader listens before they speak. Reflect on how often you allow others to share their thoughts.

5. Deceitful

Pride can make people deceitful. They may lie to protect their image or gain advantage. Dishonesty breaks trust and damages relationships. It creates confusion and leads to conflict. God calls us to live with integrity and truth. **Proverbs 11:3** says, *"The integrity of the upright guides them."* Humility helps us be honest, even when it's hard. Deceit is a sign of fear, not strength. Truth builds respect and peace. A humble heart chooses honesty over image. Living truthfully brings freedom and clarity. Think about whether your words reflect truth or pride.

6. Doubting Others

Pride leads people to unfairly doubt others. They may believe only they can do things right. This attitude discourages and disrespects others. It blocks teamwork and growth. God teaches us to think wisely and humbly. **Romans 12:3** says, *"Think of yourself with sober judgment."* Humility recognizes the value of everyone's contribution. Doubting others shows insecurity, not wisdom. Encouragement builds confidence and unity. A humble person lifts others up, not down. Trusting others is part of loving well. Consider how you view the abilities of those around you.

7. Dismissive

Pride makes people dismissive of others. They may ignore feelings, ideas, or concerns. This behavior creates hurt and distance. Dismissiveness breaks connection and trust. God calls us to listen and care deeply. **Proverbs 18:13** says, *"To answer before listening— that is folly and shame."* Humility listens with patience and love. It values every voice and heart. Being dismissive shows pride, not compassion. A humble spirit brings healing and respect. Listening is a gift we give to others. Think about how often you truly hear what others are saying.

8. Disrespect

Pride often leads people to disrespect others. A proud person may look down on those around them, thinking they are better or more important. This attitude causes them to ignore others' opinions and dismiss their feelings. Their words and actions can make others feel small and unworthy. Such behavior damages relationships and creates tension. **Proverbs 16:18** warns, *"Pride goes before destruction, a haughty spirit before a fall."* Prideful actions not only hurt individuals but also poison the atmosphere around them. When pride rules, kindness fades and division grows. But humility brings healing and connection. It helps us value others and treat them with honor. Respect grows when pride is replaced with grace. Take time to consider how your attitude affects the people around you.

9. Distance

Pride creates emotional distance between people. A proud person may believe they don't need anyone else. They avoid asking for help and keep others at arm's length. This leads to isolation and loneliness, even in moments of success. Pride also makes it hard for others to approach or connect with them. **Proverbs 18:1** says, *"An unfriendly person pursues selfish ends and, against all sound judgment, starts quarrels."* Pride builds walls that block love, support, and friendship. It stops us from sharing our struggles and receiving comfort. Humility, on the other hand, opens the door to connection. It allows us to build strong, meaningful relationships. When we choose humility, we invite others into our lives. Think about whether pride is keeping you from the people who care.

SYAVIHA MULENGYA

6

How to Make a Difference

You don't need to be famous or powerful to make a difference. God can use anyone who is willing to love and serve others with a humble heart. The Bible says, *"Let your light shine before others, that they may see your good deeds and glorify your Father in heaven"* (**Matthew 5:16**). Even small acts of kindness—like helping someone, forgiving, or simply listening—can show God's love and bring hope to others. Jesus showed us that true greatness comes through serving, not seeking attention. Making a difference starts with living for God and caring for people. When we follow Jesus' example, we become part of His plan to heal and bless the world. You don't have to do big things—just be faithful in the small ones. God sees every loving act and uses it to touch lives. When you live with purpose, humility, and love, your life becomes a light in someone's darkness, and that's how you truly make a difference.

Be the Change

1. Serve

Greatness begins with serving others. Jesus taught us that true greatness comes from serving, not being served. **Mark 10:45** says, *"For even the Son of Man did not come to be served, but to serve, und lu yive his life as a ransom for many."* Serving others means putting their needs before your own and helping them succeed.

Serving others creates a positive impact on those around you. It develops a sense of community and support, making everyone feel valued and appreciated. When you serve, you build strong relationships and create a culture of mutual respect. **Philippians 2:3-4** advises, *"Do nothing out of selfish ambition or vain conceit. Rather, in humility value others above yourselves."*

Serving also helps you grow personally. It teaches you empathy, compassion, and selflessness. By serving others, you develop qualities that contribute to your own greatness. Remember, as Jesus said in **Matthew 23:11**, *"The greatest among you will be your servant."*

2. Stay Humble

Staying humble is essential for greatness. Humility means recognizing your strengths and weaknesses and valuing others' contributions. **Proverbs 22:4** says, *"Humility is the fear of the Lord; its wages are riches and honor and life."* Humility keeps you grounded and focused on continuous improvement.

Humility develops positive relationships. When you are humble, you listen to others and appreciate their perspectives. This creates a sense of unity and cooperation. **James 4:10** reminds us, *"Humble yourselves before the Lord, and he will lift you up."* Humility earns you respect and admiration from others.

Staying humble also helps you avoid the pitfalls of pride. Pride can lead to arrogance and isolation, while humility keeps you open to learning and growth. **Proverbs 11:2** states, "*When pride comes, then comes disgrace, but with humility comes wisdom.*" Embrace humility to achieve true greatness.

3. Seek Advice

Seeking advice is a sign of wisdom and humility. **Proverbs 15:22** advises, "*Plans fail for lack of counsel, but with many advisers they succeed.*" Seeking advice means recognizing that you don't have all the answers and being open to learning from others.

Seeking advice helps you make better decisions. It allows you to consider different perspectives and gain valuable insights. When you seek advice, you show respect for others' knowledge and experience. **Proverbs 12:15** says, "*The way of fools seems right to them, but the wise listen to advice.*"

Seeking advice also leads to collaboration and teamwork. It creates a culture of mutual support and learning. By seeking advice, you build strong relationships and create a positive environment where everyone can thrive. Embrace the wisdom of others to achieve greatness.

4. Support

Supporting others is a key aspect of greatness. **Galatians 6:2** encourages, "*Carry each other's burdens, and in this way you will fulfill the law of Christ.*" Supporting others means offering help and encouragement, making them feel valued and appreciated.

Supporting others creates a positive impact on those around you. It fosters a sense of community and mutual respect. When you support others, you build strong relationships and create a culture of kindness and compassion. **Philippians 2:4** advises, "*Not looking to your own interests but each of you to the interests of the others.*"

Supporting others also helps you grow personally. It teaches you empathy, compassion, and selflessness. By supporting others, you develop qualities that contribute to your own greatness. Remember, as Jesus said in **John 15:12**, "*My command is this: Love each other as I have loved you.*"

5. Solve Problems

Solving problems is a sign of greatness. **Proverbs 3:5-6** advises, "Trust in the Lord with all your heart and lean not on your own understanding; in all your ways submit to him, and he will make your paths straight." Solving problems means finding solutions and overcoming challenges.

Solving problems helps you grow personally and professionally. It teaches you critical thinking, creativity, and resilience. When you solve problems, you develop qualities that contribute to your own greatness. **James 1:5** says, "*If any of you lacks wisdom, you should ask God, who gives generously to all without finding fault, and it will be given to you.*"

Solving problems also creates a positive impact on those around you. It leads to a sense of innovation and progress. By solving problems, you build strong relationships and create a culture of collaboration and teamwork. Embrace problem-solving to achieve greatness.

6. Search for Knowledge

Searching for knowledge is essential for greatness. **Proverbs 9:9** says, "*Instruct the wise and they will be wiser still; teach the righteous and they will add to their learning.*" Searching for knowledge means being open to learning and growing continuously.

Searching for knowledge helps you make better decisions and gain valuable insights. It allows you to consider different perspectives and stay informed. When you search for knowledge, you show respect for others' expertise and experience. **Proverbs 18:15** advises, *"The heart of the discerning acquires knowledge, for the ears of the wise seek it out."*

Searching for knowledge also leads to personal growth and development. It keeps you humble and open to new ideas. By searching for knowledge, you develop qualities that contribute to your own greatness. Embrace continuous learning to achieve greatness.

7. Submit Before God and People

Submitting before God and people is a sign of humility and greatness. **James 4:7** advises, *"Submit yourselves, then, to God. Resist the devil, and he will flee from you."* Submitting means recognizing your limitations and seeking guidance from a higher power and others.

Submitting before God helps you stay grounded and focused on what truly matters. It allows you to trust in divine support and seek wisdom. **Proverbs 3:5-6** says, *"Trust in the Lord with all your heart and lean not on your own understanding; in all your ways submit to him, and he will make your paths straight."* Submitting before people leads to positive relationships and collaboration. Embrace submission to achieve greatness.

8. Speak Well and Weigh Your Words

Speaking well and weighing your words is essential for greatness. **Proverbs 15:1** advises, *"A gentle answer turns away wrath, but a harsh word stirs up anger."* Speaking well means communicating effectively and thoughtfully.

Speaking well helps you build strong relationships and create a positive impact on those around you. When you weigh your words, you show consideration for others' feelings and perspectives. **Proverbs 16:24** says, *"Gracious words are a honeycomb, sweet to the soul and healing to the bones."*

Speaking well also helps you avoid misunderstandings and conflicts. It teaches you empathy and patience. By speaking well, you develop qualities that contribute to your own greatness. Embrace thoughtful communication to achieve greatness.

9. Sacrifice

Sacrifice is a sign of greatness. **John 15:13** says, *"Greater love has no one than this: to lay down one's life for one's friends."* Sacrifice means putting others' needs before your own and making personal sacrifices for the greater good.

Sacrifice creates a positive impact on those around you. It fosters a sense of selflessness and compassion. When you sacrifice, you build strong relationships and create a culture of kindness and support. **Philippians 2:3-4** advises, *"Do nothing out of selfish ambition or vain conceit. Rather, in humility value others above yourselves."*

Sacrifice also helps you grow personally. It teaches you empathy, compassion, and selflessness. By sacrificing, you develop qualities that contribute to your own greatness. Embrace sacrifice to achieve true greatness.

10. Separate Yourself from Negative Practices, Places, and People

Separating yourself from negative practices, places, and people is essential for greatness. **Proverbs 4:14-15** advises, *"Do not set foot on the path of the wicked or walk in the way of evildoers. Avoid* it, do not travel on it; turn from it and go on your way." Separating means distancing yourself from harmful influences.

Separating yourself from negativity helps you stay focused on positive growth and development. It allows you to avoid distractions and stay true to your values. When you separate yourself from negative influences, you create a positive environment for yourself and others. **1 Corinthians 15:33** says, *"Do not be misled: 'Bad company corrupts good character.'"* Greatness is achieved through humility, service, wisdom, and positive actions. By embracing these principles, you can create a positive impact on yourself and others. Remember, as **Proverbs 22:4** says, *"Humility is the fear of the Lord; its wages are riches and honor and life."* Let these principles guide your actions and interactions, and you will find true greatness.

The Quiet Strength That Changes the World

1. Inspires

Humility inspires others by setting a positive example. When you are humble, you show that greatness comes from serving and valuing others. This attitude encourages those around you to adopt similar behaviors. People are drawn to humble leaders who lead by example and prioritize others' well-being. As **Proverbs 27:2** says, *"Let someone else praise you, and not your own mouth; an outsider, and not your own lips."* Humility creates a ripple effect, inspiring others to act with kindness and respect. By being humble, you inspire greatness in those around you.

2. Includes

Humility includes everyone, developing a sense of belonging and unity. A humble person values others' contributions and ensures everyone feels heard and appreciated. This inclusive attitude creates a supportive and collaborative environment. As **Philippians 2:3-4** advises, *"Do nothing out of selfish ambition or vain conceit. Rather, in humility value others above yourselves."* Including others helps build strong relationships and a cohesive community. Humility breaks down barriers and promotes equality. By being inclusive, you create a positive impact on those around you.

3. Improves

Humility improves personal growth and development. When you are humble, you are open to feedback and willing to learn from others. This openness allows you to continuously improve and grow. **Proverbs 12:15** says, *"The way of fools seems right to them, but the wise listen to advice."* Humility helps you recognize your strengths and weaknesses, leading to self-improvement. By embracing humility, you become a better version of yourself. Continuous improvement is a key aspect of achieving greatness.

4. Invites

Humility invites collaboration and teamwork. A humble person seeks input from others and values their ideas. This attitude leads to a sense of cooperation and mutual respect. **Proverbs 15:22** advises, *"Plans fail for lack of counsel, but with many advisers they succeed."* Inviting others to contribute creates a positive and productive environment. Humility encourages open dialogue and shared decision-making. By inviting collaboration, you achieve better results and build stronger relationships.

5. Increases

Humility increases respect and admiration from others. When you are humble, people appreciate your genuine and selfless attitude. This respect leads to stronger relationships and greater influence. **James 4:10** reminds us, "*Humble yourselves before the Lord, and he will lift you up.*" Humility also increases your ability to learn and grow, as you are open to new ideas and perspectives. By being humble, you earn the trust and respect of those around you. Increased respect is a key aspect of achieving greatness.

6. Identifies

Humility identifies areas for improvement and growth. A humble person is self-aware and recognizes their strengths and weaknesses. This self-awareness allows for continuous development and learning. **Proverbs 15:33** says, "*Wisdom's instruction is to fear the Lord, and humility comes before honor.*" Identifying areas for improvement helps you become a better version of yourself. Humility encourages honest self-reflection and growth. By identifying your weaknesses, you can work on them and achieve greatness.

7. Invests

Humility invests in relationships and community. A humble person values others' well-being and seeks to build strong connections. This investment creates a supportive and caring environment. **Galatians 6:2** encourages, "*Carry each other's burdens, and in this way you will fulfill the law of Christ.*" Investing in relationships leads to mutual respect and trust. Humility encourages you to give your time and resources to help others. By investing in your community, you create a positive impact and achieve greatness.

8. Involves

Humility involves others in decision-making and problem-solving. A humble person seeks input and values the contributions of those around them. This involvement fosters a sense of ownership and collaboration. **Proverbs 11:14** advises, "*For lack of guidance a nation falls, but victory is won through many advisers.*" Involving others creates a positive and productive environment. Humility encourages shared responsibility and teamwork. By involving others, you achieve better results and build stronger relationships.

7

---·⟨≈⟩·---

Humble Habits For Happiness And Harmony

Happiness and harmony don't come from having everything we want—they come from how we live each day. When we choose to be humble, we stop competing and start connecting. Humility helps us listen more, speak gently, and treat others with kindness. These small choices—like saying "I'm sorry," helping without being asked, or letting someone else go first—build peace in our hearts and in our homes. The Bible says, *"Clothe yourselves with humility toward one another"* (**1 Peter 5:5**). Just like we get dressed every morning, we can choose to wear humility daily.

When we live this way, we feel lighter inside. We stop carrying pride, anger, and stress. Humble habits help us forgive quickly, stay calm in conflict, and enjoy simple things with a thankful heart. That's where real happiness begins—not in loud success, but in quiet strength. And harmony follows when we stop trying to win and start trying to love. Jesus said, *"Blessed are the peacemakers, for they will be called children of God"* (**Matthew 5:9**). When we practice humility, we become peacemakers—bringing joy to ourselves and peace to those around us.

1. Admit Your Mistakes

Admitting your mistakes is a key aspect of humility. When you acknowledge your errors, you show that you are willing to learn and grow. **Proverbs 28:13** says, *"Whoever conceals their sins does not prosper, but the one who confesses and renounces them finds mercy."* Admitting mistakes helps you take responsibility for your actions and make amends.

Admitting mistakes also leads to trust and respect. People appreciate honesty and are more likely to support you when you are open about your shortcomings. This openness creates a positive environment where everyone feels valued. **James 5:16** advises, *"Therefore confess your sins to each other and pray for each other so that you may be healed."*

Admitting mistakes is essential for personal growth. It allows you to learn from your experiences and avoid repeating the same errors. By embracing humility and admitting your mistakes, you can improve yourself and build stronger relationships. **Proverbs 12:1** says, *"Whoever loves discipline loves knowledge, but whoever hates correction is stupid."*

2. Appreciate and Show Gratitude

Appreciating and expressing gratitude are powerful ways to practice humility. When you express gratitude, you acknowledge the contributions of others and the blessings in your life. **1 Thessalonians 5:18** says, *"Give thanks in all circumstances; for this is God's will for you in Christ Jesus."* Gratitude helps you stay grounded and focused on the positive aspects of life.

Showing gratitude leads to positive relationships. People feel valued and appreciated when you acknowledge their efforts and kindness. This creates a supportive and loving environment. **Colossians 3:15** advises, *"Let the peace of Christ rule in your hearts, since as members of one body you were called to peace. And be thankful."*

Gratitude also enhances your well-being. It helps you maintain a positive outlook and reduces stress. By practicing humility and showing gratitude, you can improve your mental and emotional health. **Philippians 4:6-7** says, *"Do not be anxious about anything, but in every situation, by prayer and petition, with thanksgiving, present your requests to God."*

3. Accept Advice

Accepting advice is a sign of humility and wisdom. When you seek and accept advice, you show that you are open to learning from others. **Proverbs 19:20** says, *"Listen to advice and accept discipline, and at the end you will be counted among the wise."* Accepting advice helps you make better decisions and avoid mistakes.

Accepting advice leads to collaboration and teamwork. It shows that you value others' opinions and expertise. This creates a positive environment where everyone feels respected and appreciated. **Proverbs 12:15** advises, *"The way of fools seems right to them, but the wise listen to advice."*

Accepting advice also promotes personal growth. It allows you to gain new insights and perspectives, helping you improve yourself. By practicing humility and accepting advice, you can achieve greater success and build stronger relationships. **Proverbs 15:22** says, *"Plans fail for lack of counsel, but with many advisers they succeed."*

4. Ask Questions

Asking questions is a key aspect of humility. When you ask questions, you show that you are eager to learn and understand. **Proverbs 4:7** says, *"The beginning of wisdom is this: Get wisdom. Though it cost all you have, get understanding."* Asking questions helps you gain knowledge and improve your skills.

Asking questions fosters curiosity and growth. It encourages you to explore new ideas and seek answers. This openness to learning creates a positive environment where everyone feels encouraged to share their knowledge. **James 1:5** advises, *"If any of you lacks wisdom, you should ask God, who gives generously to all without finding fault, and it will be given to you."*

Asking questions also builds strong relationships. People appreciate it when you show interest in their thoughts and experiences. By practicing humility and asking questions, you can create meaningful connections and foster mutual respect. **Proverbs 18:15** says, *"The heart of the discerning acquires knowledge, for the ears of the wise seek it out."*

5. Apologize

Apologizing is a powerful way to practice humility. When you apologize, you acknowledge your mistakes and seek to make amends. **Matthew 5:23-24** says, *"Therefore, if you are offering your gift at the altar and there remember that your brother or sister has something against you, leave your gift there in front of the altar. First go and be reconciled to them; then come and offer your gift."* Apologizing helps heal relationships and restore trust.

Apologizing leads to forgiveness and understanding. It shows that you are willing to take responsibility for your actions and make things right. This openness creates a positive environment where everyone feels valued and respected. **Colossians 3:13** advises, *"Bear with each other and forgive one another if any of you has a grievance against someone. Forgive as the Lord forgave you."*

Apologizing also promotes personal growth. It allows you to learn from your mistakes and avoid repeating them. By practicing humility and apologizing, you can improve yourself and build stronger relationships. **Proverbs 28:13** says, *"Whoever conceals their sins does not prosper, but the one who confesses and renounces them finds mercy."*

6. Admire Others

Admiring others is a sign of humility. When you admire others, you recognize their strengths and achievements. **Romans 12:10** says, *"Be devoted to one another in love. Honor one another above yourselves."* Admiring others helps you appreciate their contributions and value their efforts.

Admiring others brings positive relationships. People feel valued and appreciated when you acknowledge their strengths and achievements. This creates a supportive and loving environment. **Philippians 2:3** advises, *"Do nothing out of selfish ambition or vain conceit. Rather, in humility value others above yourselves."*

Admiring others also promotes personal growth. It encourages you to learn from their strengths and strive to improve yourself. By practicing humility and admiring others, you can create a positive impact on those around you. **Proverbs 27:17** says, *"As iron sharpens iron, so one person sharpens another."*

7. Avoid Boasting

Avoiding boasting is essential for practicing humility. Boasting can create a sense of arrogance and superiority. **Proverbs 27:2** advises, *"Let someone else praise you, and not your own mouth; an outsider, and not your own lips."* Avoiding boasting helps you stay grounded and focused on genuine achievements.

Avoiding boasting leads to positive relationships. People appreciate humility and are more likely to support you when you are modest about your accomplishments. This creates a respectful and supportive environment. **James 4:6** says, *"God opposes the proud but shows favor to the humble."*

Avoiding boasting also promotes personal growth. It allows you to focus on continuous improvement rather than seeking validation from others. By practicing humility and avoiding boasting, you can build stronger relationships and achieve true greatness. **Proverbs 16:18** warns, *"Pride goes before destruction, a haughty spirit before a fall."*

8. Attend to Others

Attending to others is a key aspect of humility. When you attend to others, you show that you care about their well-being and needs. **Philippians 2:4** advises, *"Not looking to your own interests but each of you to the interests of the others."* Attending to others helps create a supportive and caring environment.

Attending to others creates positive relationships. People feel valued and appreciated when you show concern for their needs and well-being. This creates a sense of community and mutual respect. **Galatians 6:2** encourages, *"Carry each other's burdens, and in this way you will fulfill the law of Christ."*

Attending to others also promotes personal growth. It teaches you empathy, compassion, and selflessness. By practicing humility and attending to others, you can create a positive impact on those around you. **Proverbs 11:25** says, *"A generous person will prosper; whoever refreshes others will be refreshed."*

9. Answer Well with Kindness

Answering well with kindness is essential for practicing humility. When you respond to others with kindness, you show respect and consideration for their feelings. **Proverbs 15:1** advises, *"A gentle answer turns away wrath, but a harsh word stirs up anger."* Answering well with kindness helps create a positive and respectful environment.

Answering well with kindness promotes positive relationships. People appreciate it when you respond thoughtfully and kindly, even in difficult situations. This creates a sense of trust and mutual respect. **Ephesians 4:29** says, *"Do not let any unwholesome talk come out of your mouths, but only what is helpful for building others up according to their needs, that it may benefit those who listen."*

Answering well with kindness also promotes personal growth. It teaches you patience, empathy, and effective communication. By practicing humility and answering well with kindness, you can build stronger relationships and create a positive impact on those around you. **Proverbs 16:24** says, *"Gracious words are a honeycomb, sweet to the soul and healing to the bones."*

10. Assess Your Life

Assessing your life is a powerful way to practice humility. Reflecting on your actions and decisions helps you gain insight into your strengths and weaknesses. **Lamentations 3:40** says, *"Let us* *examine our ways and test them, and let us return to the Lord."* Assessing your life helps you identify areas for improvement and growth.

Assessing your life develops self-awareness and personal growth. It allows you to learn from your experiences and make positive changes. This self-reflection creates a sense of accountability and responsibility. **Proverbs 4:26** advises, *"Give careful thought to the paths for your feet and be steadfast in all your ways."*

8

Humble Living, Happy Life

The Path to Inner Healing and Peace of Mind

Humility is more than modesty—it's a quiet strength that opens the door to healing. When we let go of pride, comparison, and the need to be right, we make space for grace to enter. The Bible reminds us in **James 4:6**, *"God opposes the proud but gives grace to the humble."* That grace brings inner healing. Humility allows us to face our weaknesses without shame and accept help without fear. It softens our hearts, calms our thoughts, and helps us forgive ourselves and others. In humility, we stop striving to prove our worth and begin to rest in God's love.

Peace of mind flows naturally from a humble spirit. When we stop chasing approval and start trusting God's plan, anxiety loses its grip. **Philippians 4:6-7** encourages us, *"Do not be anxious about anything… and the peace of God, which transcends all understanding, will guard your hearts and your minds in Christ Jesus."* Humility teaches us to surrender control, to live simply, and to love deeply. It brings harmony to our relationships and clarity to our thoughts. In a world full of noise and pressure, humility is the quiet path that leads us home—to healing, peace, and joy.

1. Gratitude

Humility leads to gratitude by helping you recognize the contributions of others and the blessings in your life. When you are humble, you appreciate the kindness and support you receive from those around you. This sense of gratitude enhances your mental well-being, making you feel more content and positive. As **1 Thessalonians 5:18** says, *"Give thanks in all circumstances; for this is God's will for you in Christ Jesus."*

Gratitude also helps you focus on the positive aspects of life, reducing stress and anxiety. When you practice humility and express gratitude, you shift your attention away from negative thoughts and towards the good things you have. This positive mindset improves your overall mental health. **Philippians 4:6-7** advises, *"Do not be anxious about anything, but in every situation, by prayer and petition, with thanksgiving, present your requests to God."*

Humility and gratitude create a cycle of positivity. As you appreciate others and the blessings in your life, you become more humble, and this humility further enhances your gratitude. By practicing humility and gratitude daily, you can improve your mental health and create a positive impact on yourself and those around you.

2. Growth

Humility promotes personal growth by encouraging you to learn from your experiences and seek improvement. When you are humble, you recognize your strengths and weaknesses and are open to feedback. This openness allows you to continuously grow and develop. **Proverbs 12:1** says, *"Whoever loves discipline loves knowledge, but whoever hates correction is stupid."*

Personal growth is essential for mental health. It helps you build resilience and adaptability, making it easier to cope with challenges. Humility fosters a growth mindset, where you see setbacks as opportunities to learn and grow. This positive approach enhances your mental well-being. **James 1:5** advises, *"If any of you lacks wisdom, you should ask God, who gives generously to all without finding fault, and it will be given to you."*

Humility also helps you build strong relationships that support your growth. When you are humble, you seek advice and learn from others, creating a network of support and encouragement. By embracing humility and focusing on personal growth, you can improve your mental health and achieve greater success.

3. Generosity

Humility encourages generosity by making you more aware of others' needs. When you are humble, you prioritize helping and supporting those around you. This generosity creates a sense of fulfillment and purpose, enhancing your mental well-being. **Acts 20:35** says, *"It is more blessed to give than to receive."* When you give to others, you build trust and create a supportive community. This sense of connection and belonging improves your mental health. **Proverbs 11:25** advises, *"A generous person will prosper; whoever refreshes others will be refreshed."*

Humility and generosity bring kindness. As you give to others, you become more humble, and this humility further enhances your generosity. By practicing humility and generosity daily, you can improve your mental health and create a positive impact on yourself and those around you.

4. Genuineness

Humility goes hand in hand with genuineness, encouraging you to be true to yourself and to others. When you are humble, you are honest about your strengths and weaknesses and avoid pretending to be someone you are not. This authenticity enhances your mental well-being, making you feel more confident and secure. **Proverbs 12:22** says, "*The Lord detests lying lips, but he delights in people who are trustworthy.*"

Genuineness also helps you build strong relationships based on trust and respect. When you are genuine, people appreciate your honesty and are more likely to support you. This sense of connection and trust improves your mental health. **Ephesians 4:25** advises, "*Therefore each of you must put off falsehood and speak truthfully to your neighbor, for we are all members of one body.*"

Humility and genuineness create a cycle of authenticity. As you embrace humility, you become more genuine, and this authenticity further enhances your humility. By practicing humility and genuineness daily, you can improve your mental health and create a positive impact on yourself and those around you.

5. Gentleness

Humility promotes gentleness by encouraging you to treat others with kindness and respect. When you are humble, you are more patient and understanding, creating a positive environment for yourself and those around you. This gentleness enhances your mental well-being, making you feel calmer and more content. **Proverbs 15:1** says, "*A gentle answer turns away wrath, but a harsh word stirs up anger.*"

Gentleness also helps you build strong relationships. When you treat others with gentleness, you create a sense of trust and mutual respect. This positive interaction improves your mental health. **Ephesians 4:2** advises, *"Be completely humble and gentle; be patient, bearing with one another in love."*

As you embrace humility, you become more gentle, and this gentleness further enhances your humility. By practicing humility and gentleness daily, you can improve your mental health and create a positive impact on yourself and those around you.

6. Giving

Humility encourages giving by making you more aware of others' needs. When you are humble, you prioritize helping and supporting those around you. This giving creates a sense of fulfillment and purpose, enhancing your mental well-being. **Luke 6:38** says, *"Give, and it will be given to you. A good measure, pressed down, shaken together and running over, will be poured into your lap."*

Giving also strengthens positive relationships. When you give to others, you build trust and create a supportive community. This sense of connection and belonging improves your mental health. **Proverbs 11:25** advises, *"A generous person will prosper; whoever refreshes others will be refreshed."* By practicing humility and giving daily, you can improve your mental health and create a positive impact on yourself and those around you.

7. Grace

Humility walks with grace by encouraging you to forgive others and yourself. When you are humble, you recognize that everyone makes mistakes and deserves compassion. This grace enhances your mental well-being, making you feel more peaceful and content. **Colossians 3:13** says, *"Bear with each other and forgive one* *another if any of you has a grievance against someone. Forgive as the Lord forgave you."*

Grace also helps you build strong relationships. **Ephesians 4:32** advises, *"Be kind and compassionate to one another, forgiving each other, just as in Christ God forgave you."* Humility and grace create compassion. As you embrace humility, you become more graceful, and this grace further enhances your humility. By practicing humility and grace daily, you can improve your mental health and create a positive impact on yourself and those around you.

8. Goodwill

Humility promotes goodwill by encouraging you to act with kindness and generosity. When you are humble, you prioritize others' well-being and seek to create a positive impact. This goodwill enhances your mental well-being, making you feel more fulfilled and content. **Galatians 6:10** says, *"Therefore, as we have opportunity, let us do good to all people, especially to those who belong to the family of believers."*

Goodwill also helps you build strong relationships. When you act with goodwill, you create a sense of trust and mutual respect. This positive interaction improves your mental health. **Proverbs 3:27** advises, *"Do not withhold good from those to whom it is due, when it is in your power to act."*

As you embrace humility, you act with goodwill, and this goodwill further enhances your humility. By practicing humility and goodwill daily, you can improve your mental health and create a positive impact on yourself and those around you.

9. Guidance

Humility encourages seeking guidance from others and from God. When you are humble, you recognize that you don't have all the answers and are open to learning from others. This guidance enhances your mental well-being, making you feel more confident and secure. **Proverbs 3:5-6** says, *"Trust in the Lord with all your heart and lean not on your own understanding; in all your ways submit to him, and he will make your paths straight."*

Seeking guidance enhances relationships. When you seek advice from others, you show respect for their knowledge and experience. This creates a supportive and collaborative environment. **Proverbs 15:22** advises, *"Plans fail for lack of counsel, but with many advisers they succeed."*

Humility and guidance create a cycle of wisdom. As you embrace humility, you seek guidance, and this guidance further enhances your humility. By practicing humility and seeking daily guidance, you can improve your mental health and have a positive impact on yourself and those around you.

10. Gladness

Humility teaches us to rejoice. When you are humble, you focus on the positive aspects of life and find contentment in being yourself. This gladness enhances your mental well-being, making you feel happier and more fulfilled. **Psalm 118:24** says, *"The Lord has done it this very day; let us rejoice today and be glad."* Gladness also helps you build strong relationships. When you are glad, you create a positive and uplifting environment for yourself and those around you. This sense of joy improves your mental health.

9

---·⟨~⟩·---

Building Healthy And Happy Relationships

To build a happy and healthy relationship, we must begin with love that is patient, kind, and humble. The Bible teaches in **1 Corinthians 13:4-7**, *"Love is patient, love is kind. It does not envy, it does not boast, it is not proud... It always protects, always trusts, always hopes, always perseveres."* This kind of love creates a safe space where both people feel valued and respected. We build trust by being honest and gentle in our words—*"A gentle answer turns away wrath, but a harsh word stirs up anger"* (**Proverbs 15:1**). Forgiveness is also key. Holding grudges breaks peace, but forgiving brings healing. *"Be kind and compassionate to one another, forgiving each other, just as in Christ God forgave you"* (**Ephesians 4:32**). Listening with care, speaking with grace, and serving each other with humility are daily habits that strengthen the bond. When we put others first—*"Honor one another above yourselves"* (**Romans 12:10**)—we build relationships that reflect God's love. A happy relationship isn't perfect, but it's built on grace, truth, and a heart that chooses peace over pride every day.

SYAVIHA MULENGYA

Grow Together, Stay Strong

1. Prioritize

Prioritizing others is a key aspect of humility in relationships. When you prioritize someone, you show that their needs and feelings are important to you. This act of putting others first brings trust and respect. **Philippians 2:3-4** advises, *"Do nothing out of selfish ambition or vain conceit. Rather, in humility value others above yourselves, not looking to your own interests but each of you to the interests of the others."* By prioritizing others, you create a supportive and loving environment.

Prioritizing others also helps build strong relationships. When you make someone a priority, they feel valued and appreciated. This sense of importance strengthens the bond between you. It shows that you are willing to make sacrifices for their well-being. Proverbs 3:27 says, "Do not withhold good from those to whom it is due, when it is in your power to act." Prioritizing others is a powerful way to demonstrate humility and love.

Prioritizing others requires selflessness and empathy. It means considering their needs and feelings before your own. This selfless attitude leads to mutual respect and understanding. By practicing humility and prioritizing others, you can build meaningful, lasting relationships. Remember, as Jesus said in **Mark 12:31**, *"Love your neighbor as yourself."*

2. Pardon

Pardoning others is essential for maintaining humility in relationships. When you forgive someone, you show that you value the relationship more than holding onto grudges. Forgiveness heals and reconciles. **Colossians 3:13** advises, *"Bear with each other and forgive one another if any of you has a grievance against someone.*

Forgive as the Lord forgave you." By pardoning others, you create a positive and peaceful environment.

Forgiveness also helps build strong relationships. When you pardon someone, you demonstrate compassion and understanding. This act of mercy strengthens the relationship. **Ephesians 4:32** says, *"Be kind and compassionate to one another, forgiving each other, just as in Christ God forgave you."* Forgiveness is a powerful way to show humility and love.

Pardoning others requires letting go of anger and resentment. It means choosing to move forward and focus on the positive aspects of the relationship. This attitude creates trust and harmony. By practicing humility and pardoning others, you can build meaningful, lasting relationships. Remember, as **Matthew 6:14-15** says, *"For if you forgive other people when they sin against you, your heavenly Father will also forgive you."*

3. Praise

Praising others is a sign of humility in relationships. When you acknowledge someone's achievements and strengths, you show that you value their contributions. **Proverbs 27:2** advises, *"Let someone else praise you, and not your own mouth; an outsider, and not your own lips."* By praising others, you create a positive and uplifting environment.

Praise also helps build strong relationships. When you recognize someone's efforts, they feel valued and motivated. **Philippians 2:3** says, *"Do nothing out of selfish ambition or vain conceit. Rather, in humility value others above yourselves."* Praise is a powerful way to demonstrate humility and love.

Praising others requires genuine admiration and respect. It means acknowledging their strengths and achievements without envy or jealousy. This attitude connects to trust and encouragement. By practicing humility and praising others, you can build meaningful, lasting relationships. Remember, as **Romans 12:10** says, *"Be devoted to one another in love. Honor one another above yourselves."*

4. Participate

Participating actively in relationships is a key aspect of humility. When you engage with others, you show that you value their presence and contributions. Active participation fosters a sense of connection and collaboration. **Ecclesiastes 4:9-10** says, *"Two are better than one... If either of them falls down, one can help the other up."* By participating, you create a supportive and interactive environment.

Participation also helps build strong relationships. When you take part in activities and conversations, you demonstrate interest and commitment. **Proverbs 27:17** says, *"As iron sharpens iron, so one person sharpens another."* Participation is a powerful way to show humility and love.

Participating requires attentiveness and involvement. It means being present and actively contributing to the relationship. By practicing humility and actively participating, you can create meaningful, lasting relationships. Remember, as **Hebrews 10:24-25** says, *"And let us consider how we may spur one another on toward love and good deeds, not giving up meeting together."*

5. Provide

Providing for others is a true reflection of humility in relationships. By offering your help and support, you demonstrate genuine care for their well-being. This act of generosity creates a sense of safety and trust. **Galatians 6:2** encourages us, saying,

"Carry each other's burdens, and in this way you will fulfill the law of Christ." Supporting others in this way nurtures a caring and uplifting environment.

Additionally, providing for others strengthens bonds and leads to mutual respect. When you extend assistance, you help others feel valued and appreciated. **Proverbs 11:25** says, "A generous person will prosper; whoever refreshes others will be refreshed." By stepping in to help, you bring positivity and love into your relationships.

Generosity and compassion are vital when it comes to providing for others. Sharing your time and resources with those in need not only reflects humility but also builds strong and meaningful connections. As **1 John 3:17** reminds us, "If anyone has material possessions and sees a brother or sister in need but has no pity on them, how can the love of God be in that person?" Through acts of provision, we embody the essence of kindness and empathy.

6. Pause

Taking the time to pause and listen is crucial for building humility in relationships. When you truly listen, you show that you value others' feelings and perspectives. This attentiveness nurtures understanding and respect. **James 1:19** advises, "Everyone should be quick to listen, slow to speak and slow to become angry." By being present and giving others your attention, you create a harmonious and considerate atmosphere.

Pausing also allows you to reflect on your words and actions. Thoughtfulness strengthens relationships by showing others that you care about how your behavior affects them. **Proverbs 15:1** states, "A gentle answer turns away wrath, but a harsh word stirs up anger." Practicing mindfulness in this way creates deeper connections and promotes trust.

Exercising patience and attentiveness is key to pausing effectively. By taking a moment to reflect and understand others, you cultivate empathy and create stronger, more meaningful relationships. **Proverbs 18:13** reminds us, *"To answer before listening—that is folly and shame."* In your relationships, pausing opens the door to deeper understanding and connection.

7. Pacify

Resolving conflicts peacefully is a powerful expression of humility in relationships. When you address disagreements with patience and understanding, you show your commitment to harmony and mutual respect. **Matthew 5:9** says, *"Blessed are the peacemakers, for they will be called children of God."* Taking a peaceful approach ensures that relationships remain positive and are built on trust.

Dealing with conflicts calmly strengthens bonds and encourages compassion. **Proverbs 15:18** teaches, *"A hot-tempered person stirs up conflict, but the one who is patient calms a quarrel."* Choosing to pacify conflicts shows your willingness to prioritize unity and mutual understanding over discord.

Patience and a willingness to find common ground are essential for resolving conflicts. By being empathetic and open to dialogue, you lay the foundation for trust and cooperation. **Romans 12:18** states, *"If it is possible, as far as it depends on you, live at peace with everyone."* Practicing humility in this way brings lasting harmony to your relationships.

8. Permit

Allowing others to express themselves freely is an important aspect of humility in relationships. When you encourage open communication, you show that you respect their perspectives and value their individuality. **Proverbs 18:2** says, *"Fools find no pleasure in understanding but delight in airing their own opinions."* By giving others the space to share their thoughts, you foster inclusiveness and mutual respect.

Open communication builds trust and strengthens relationships. When others feel heard and understood, they are more likely to connect with you on a deeper level. **James 1:19** reminds us, *"Everyone should be quick to listen, slow to speak and slow to become angry."* Encouraging expression is a meaningful way to show kindness and love.

Practicing openness requires attentiveness and genuine curiosity. By embracing others' viewpoints, you create an atmosphere of trust and understanding. **Proverbs 18:13** teaches, *"To answer before listening—that is folly and shame."* In relationships, granting permission to express oneself strengthens the bond and promotes empathy.

9. Protect

Protecting others is a meaningful way to show humility and love in relationships. When you safeguard someone's well-being, you demonstrate care and commitment to their happiness and security. **Psalm 82:3-4** urges, *"Defend the weak and the fatherless; uphold the cause of the poor and the oppressed. Rescue the weak and the needy; deliver them from the hand of the wicked."* Through acts of protection, you create a caring and supportive environment.

SYAVIHA MULENGYA

Taking steps to protect others strengthens trust and deepens connections. When people feel safe with you, they are more likely to open up and rely on you for support. This responsibility reflects compassion and empathy.

Protecting others requires courage and a willingness to prioritize their safety and needs. By stepping up when it matters, you embody the qualities of humility and kindness. In doing so, you foster relationships built on love, respect, and enduring care.

Speak Gently, Love Deeply

Humility is the secret to living a life you love because it transforms how you see yourself, others, and the world around you. When you are humble, you no longer focus on proving yourself or competing with others. Instead, humility helps you appreciate the blessings God has placed in your life—your family, friends, and the opportunities you have to grow and serve. It teaches you to value people for who they are, not for what they can do for you. Humility creates harmony and removes pride, which often leads to selfishness and conflict. The Bible says in **Micah 6:8**, "*Act justly, love mercy, and walk humbly with your God.*" This verse reminds us that humility is not only pleasing to God but also a pathway to a peaceful and meaningful life. It takes away the struggles that come with arrogance and replaces them with gratitude, kindness, and love.

Humility opens your heart to relationships that bring true joy. When you humble yourself, you become a better listener, a more compassionate friend, and a forgiving person. Humility removes the need for bitterness or resentment and helps you find peace with others. You learn to walk in God's love and to share it with those around you, lifting them up rather than tearing them down. Humility also frees you from the stress of comparison and allows you to focus on the good in your life. The Bible teaches in **James**

4:10, *"Humble yourselves before the Lord, and he will lift you up."* When you live with humility, God blesses you with strength, wisdom, and grace. This attitude of humility leads to a life filled with joy, peace, and fulfillment—a life you truly love and cherish.

Humility is the key to living a contented and joyful life because it shapes your mindset and transforms how you experience the world. First, humility helps you see the blessings God has given you—from the smallest gifts to the most significant opportunities—encouraging gratitude and peace in your heart. **Proverbs 22:4** reminds us, *"Humility is the fear of the Lord; its wages are riches and honor and life."* Second, it reduces complaints by shifting your focus from dissatisfaction to thankfulness, allowing you to enjoy the present without frustration.

Third, humility helps you overcome pride, which often leads to conflict and unhappiness, replacing it with kindness, respect, and harmony. **James 4:6** says, *"God opposes the proud but shows favor to the humble,"* showing the importance of humility in leading a peaceful life. Fourth, humility strengthens your dependence on God by acknowledging that you need His wisdom and guidance, bringing peace and reassurance. **Psalm 25:9** says, *"He guides the humble in what is right and teaches them His way."* Finally, humility helps you connect more deeply with people, encouraging patience, forgiveness, and love, which builds stronger relationships. **Ephesians 4:2** teaches, *"Be completely humble and gentle; be patient, bearing with one another in love."* Through humility, you experience gratitude, peace, and love, leading to a life of true contentment and joy.

10

Make Life Beautiful

Serving others is one of the most meaningful ways to live a life of greatness and significance. My late mother, Elisabeth, often encouraged me to love serving. She would say, "Through serving, you find your miracle." Her words have proven to be true many times. I remember when someone asked me to duplicate music music video. While checking the quality, I noticed a lady singing on one of the recordings, and that is how I met my wife. If I had refused to serve, I might have missed that life-changing moment. Serving opens doors to unexpected blessings and opportunities.

Serving others is more than an act of kindness—it is a way to make life beautiful, blessed, and better. When we serve, we honor God and fulfill the purpose He has placed in our lives. In **Galatians 6:9,** it says, *"Let us not become weary in doing good, for at the proper time we will reap a harvest if we do not give up."* Service has the power to bring joy and hope to both the giver and receiver. It allows us to share God's love and make a positive impact on others' lives.

SYAVIHA MULENGYA

Through serving, we create stronger relationships and promote growth. Acts of service build trust and deepen bonds between people, reminding them that they are valued. **Proverbs 11:25** teaches, "*A generous person will prosper; whoever refreshes others will be refreshed.*" Service has a way of enriching our lives and the lives of those we serve, inspiring both personal and collective progress.

Serving others also reflects the greatness within us. Jesus Himself taught the importance of serving when He washed His disciples' feet, saying in **John 13:14**, "*Now that I, your Lord and Teacher, have washed your feet, you also should wash one another's feet.*" Serving reminds us to live with humility and love, lifting others up and making the world a brighter and kinder place.

Serving others is one of the most powerful ways to live a meaningful and impactful life. When you give your time, effort, and love to help those in need, you fulfill your calling to live, love, lead, and light up the world. Acts of service can strengthen hearts and bring lasting change to the lives you touch. As Jesus said in **Matthew 5:16**, "*Let your light shine before others, that they may see your good deeds and glorify your Father in heaven.*" Serving is not just about what you can do for others; it is an opportunity to discover more about yourself. Through service, you begin to understand your abilities, your worth, and the unique gifts God has placed within you.

One of the lessons you learn through serving is the value of your talents and purpose. God has given each of us special abilities to make a difference in the world, and serving allows us to use these gifts for good. **Romans 12:6-7** says, "*We have different gifts, according to the grace given to each of us. If your gift is serving, then serve; if it is teaching, then teach.*" Serving helps you recognize your potential and the impact you can make. Another lesson is that service teaches resilience and growth. When you step out of your comfort zone to help someone, you develop courage, adaptability, and strength. **Philippians 4:13** reminds us, "*I can do all this through Him who gives me strength.*" Service reveals the greatness that lies within you and reminds you of your ability to make a positive impact.

Serving others is a reflection of humility and love. It helps you connect deeply with others, appreciate their struggles, and offer meaningful support. In **Galatians 5:13**, it says, "*Serve one another humbly in love.*" Through service, you also build relationships that matter, creating a network of trust and encouragement. Each act of service brings you closer to your purpose, aligning your life with the calling to make a difference. Greatness is not about fame or recognition—it is about touching lives and making the world better. By serving others, you fulfill your mission and discover the incredible blessings that God has prepared for you. Let your service be an example of dedication and love that inspires others to follow the path of significance.

Making Life Beautiful Through Servant Leadership

Serving others is an important lesson taught in the Bible. Jesus, the best example of a servant leader, showed us how to care for people selflessly and with love. In today's world, where selfishness and greed often cause pain, we need servant leaders to bring hope and joy.

A servant leader is someone who cares more about helping others than gaining power or wealth. This chapter talks about how serving others can change lives and make the world a better place. It starts with serving those closest to us and grows to serving others in the community.

SYAVIHA MULENGYA

The Bible reminds us that every person is valuable. Servant leadership means treating people with kindness, respect, and fairness. It is about making life brighter for everyone, not just ourselves. This is how we make life truly beautiful.

Let us explore how we can serve others and make a big difference, starting right at home and spreading out to the world.

Start Serving at Home

Serving others begins with the people closest to you—your family, friends, and community. The Bible teaches in **1 Timothy 3:5** that if we cannot take care of our own home, we cannot take care of bigger responsibilities. When we serve our family, we build love, trust, and strong relationships.

Simple acts, like helping a family member or being there to listen, are powerful. These acts make our homes places full of peace and joy. When we learn to serve the people we know, it becomes easier to serve others outside the home. As Jesus said in **Matthew 25:40**, *"Whatever you did for the least of these, you did for me."*

Serving at home prepares us to make a difference in the world. The kindness and love we practice with our families can spread to others, creating a ripple of good actions.

The World Needs Servant Leaders

The world is full of challenges and struggles. Many leaders today care only about themselves and their own gain, while the people who trusted them suffer in sadness and stress. This is why the world needs servant leaders.

A servant leader puts the needs of others first. They focus on making life better for the people they serve. The Bible tells us in **Philippians 2:3-4** to *"value others above yourself"* and to look out for their interests. This means servant leaders do not discriminate or pick favorites. They care about everyone.

By protecting others, solving problems, and keeping their promises, servant leaders bring happiness and hope. The world needs leaders who truly value people and work to make life beautiful for everyone.

Serving Brings Joy and Change

When we serve others, we bring smiles and happiness into their lives. Small things, like meeting someone's need or offering kind words, can make a big difference. The Bible encourages us in **Galatians 6:9** to *"not become tired of doing good."* Serving others spreads love and hope.

Servant leadership is not just about helping people in need. It also inspires others to help. When we serve, we show others how to be kind and caring, and it creates a chain reaction of good deeds.

Serving others also solves bigger problems in the community. A servant leader works to keep people safe, meet their needs, and support their dreams. This makes communities stronger and filled with joy.

The Beauty of Servant Leadership: A Path to Greatness

Servant Leadership Brings a Smile

A servant leader is someone who dedicates their efforts to making others happy, bringing smiles to their faces through selfless acts of kindness. Serving others with humility reminds people of their worth and helps them feel appreciated. **Proverbs 11:25** tells us, *"A generous person will prosper; whoever refreshes others will be refreshed."* This type of leadership inspires joy, creating a sense of belonging in the community.

SYAVIHA MULENGYA

Furthermore, smiles are contagious. When leaders serve genuinely, their positive energy encourages others to act with compassion. Servant leaders teach us how kindness can brighten the lives of everyone they touch. A smile might seem small, but it is a powerful gesture that can heal and unite people.

A leader who serves inspires hope in their followers, even during difficult times. Their dedication reminds people that they are not alone and that brighter days are ahead. Servant leadership is not about commanding respect but earning it through heartfelt service, proving that greatness lies in uplifting others.

1. Strengthens People

Servant leadership helps people grow stronger and more confident. By supporting others in their struggles, servant leaders provide encouragement and guidance, empowering them to face challenges with courage. **Philippians 4:13** says, "*I can do all this through Him who gives me strength.*" Servant leaders embody this, helping people overcome obstacles.

Additionally, servant leaders prioritize building others' skills and confidence. They invest in people by mentoring them, sharing wisdom, and creating opportunities for growth. This approach makes individuals and communities resilient, fostering an environment where people thrive and succeed.

By strengthening people, servant leaders create an effect of empowerment. Those who are uplifted go on to uplift others. Servant leadership proves that greatness lies not in personal power but in creating a chain of positive influence that reaches far and wide.

2. Serves Without Discrimination

True servant leadership does not favor anyone based on their status, background, or identity. Jesus taught us to love and serve all, regardless of their circumstances. **Galatians 3:28** reminds us, *"There is neither Jew nor Gentile, slave nor free, male nor female, for you are all one in Christ Jesus."* Servant leaders embrace this teaching, serving everyone equally.

This approach builds trust and leads to harmony. By serving without discrimination, leaders show that everyone matters and deserves respect. Servant leaders prioritize unity, creating a culture where diversity is celebrated and differences do not divide.

When leaders serve inclusively, they set an example that inspires others to do the same. They encourage fairness and equality, reminding people that greatness comes from lifting everyone up, not just a select few.

3. Sees the Value in Others

Servant leaders recognize the unique value and potential of every person. They treat others with dignity and respect, appreciating their individuality. **Psalm 139:14** says, *"I praise you because I am fearfully and wonderfully made; your works are wonderful."* Servant leaders honor this truth by valuing people as God's creations. This perspective helps individuals feel seen and appreciated. When leaders affirm others, they encourage them to embrace their strengths and talents. A leader who sees value in others nurtures their growth, unlocking their potential and enabling them to contribute meaningfully to society. Recognizing people's value strengthens relationships and builds trust. Servant leaders show that greatness is achieved not by seeking self-worth, but by uplifting others.

4. Supplies the Needs of Others

Servant leaders focus on meeting the needs of others, ensuring they have the resources and support to live fulfilling lives. **Matthew 25:35-36** highlights the importance of providing for others: *"For I was hungry and you gave me something to eat, I was thirsty and you gave me something to drink, I was a stranger and you invited me in."* Servant leaders follow this example, addressing the needs of the people they serve.

They work tirelessly to ensure that no one is left wanting. Servant leaders actively seek out those in need and provide tangible help, whether through food, shelter, education, or emotional support. They understand that greatness lies in generosity, not accumulation. By meeting people's needs, servant leaders build a foundation of trust and gratitude. Their actions inspire others to join the effort, creating a community where everyone supports and cares for each other.

5. Shields People

Servant leaders take responsibility for protecting those they serve, ensuring their safety and security. This mirrors the biblical calling in **Psalm 82:3-4**: *"Defend the weak and the fatherless; uphold the cause of the poor and oppressed. Rescue the weak and the needy; deliver them from the hand of the wicked."* Leaders who serve shield the vulnerable from harm and provide comfort.

They act as guardians, watching over their communities and taking action to prevent injustice. Servant leaders understand that their greatness lies in ensuring the well-being of those they serve, not in their own power.

When people feel secure under the protection of servant leaders, they gain confidence to grow and flourish. This creates a society built on trust, where individuals support one another, knowing they are protected by leaders who genuinely care.

6. Supports Others

Servant leaders actively support others, cheering them on in their endeavors and helping them achieve success. **Proverbs 27:17** says, "*As iron sharpens iron, so one person sharpens another.*" Leaders who serve strengthen and refine others, offering encouragement and practical help. This support brings collaboration, where individuals work together to achieve shared goals. Servant leaders understand that their success is intertwined with the success of those they serve, creating a culture of mutual growth. Through support, servant leaders build connections and trust. They prove that greatness lies in uplifting others and celebrating their achievements, rather than seeking personal glory.

7. Spreads Love

Servant leaders lead by love in their actions, spreading kindness and compassion wherever they go. This reflects the greatest commandment in **Matthew 22:39**: "*Love your neighbor as yourself.*" They lead with love, transforming communities and bringing healing. By spreading love, servant leaders create unity and harmony. Their actions inspire others to act with love, creating a cycle of positivity and care. Servant leadership demonstrates that greatness is rooted in compassion, not authority. Love motivates people to care deeply for one another. Servant leaders show how love can bridge divides and create an environment where everyone feels valued and uplifted.

8. Solves Problems

Servant leaders are problem solvers who work tirelessly to find solutions to the challenges their communities face. **James 1:5** reminds us, "*If any of you lacks wisdom, you should ask God, who gives generously to all without finding fault, and it will be given to you.*" Servant leaders seek God's guidance as they address issues with wisdom and integrity.

They prioritize solving problems that affect others' well-being, using creativity and collaboration to find effective solutions. Servant leaders prove that greatness lies in serving others by addressing their needs and challenges. Problem-solving fosters trust and hope. By finding solutions, servant leaders inspire others to do the same, creating a culture where challenges are met with strength and resilience.

9. Speaks and Keeps Promises

Servant leaders value integrity, speaking truthfully, and keeping their promises. **Ecclesiastes 5:5** reminds us, "*It is better not to make a vow than to make one and not fulfill it.*" Leaders who serve ensure that their words align with their actions, building trust and reliability. They understand the importance of keeping their word, as broken promises can erode trust. Servant leaders lead by example, showing that greatness is achieved through honesty and dependability.

By fulfilling promises, servant leaders create a foundation of trust and respect. Their actions inspire others to act with integrity, fostering a community built on reliability and commitment.

Servant Leadership Saves Lives

Servant leaders dedicate themselves to saving lives, both physically and emotionally. **John 15:13** says, "*Greater love has no one than this: to lay down one's life for one's friends.*" Leaders who serve prioritize the well-being of others above their own, ensuring that people feel cared for and protected.

SYAVIHA MULENGYA

They act as advocates for justice, defending those in need and preventing harm. Servant leaders understand that greatness lies in their ability to save and support others, creating a legacy of compassion.

Saving lives goes beyond physical acts—it includes lifting people from despair and giving them hope. Servant leaders inspire others to be lifesavers, creating a ripple effect of kindness that transforms the world.

10. LIVE LIKE CHRIST

Living like Christ means letting His love, humility, and truth shape every part of your life. It's not just about believing in Jesus—it's about becoming more like Him in how you think, speak, and act. Jesus lived with compassion, served others selflessly, forgave freely, and stayed close to God through prayer. To follow His example, we must choose love over judgment, grace over pride, and service over self-interest.

The Bible says, *"Whoever claims to live in Him must live as Jesus did"* (**1 John 2:6**). That means practicing humility like Jesus did when He washed His disciples' feet (**John 13:14–15**), showing mercy like He did with the woman caught in sin (**John 8:10–11**), and staying faithful in prayer like He did in the Garden of Gethsemane (**Luke 22:41–42**). Living like Christ also means forgiving others, even when it's hard—*"Forgive as the Lord forgave you"* (**Colossians 3:13**). When we walk in His footsteps, we find peace, purpose, and a deeper connection with God.

1. Wash Disciples' Feet

The secret of greatness lies in humility and service, as beautifully demonstrated by Jesus when He washed His disciples' feet. This was not an act expected of a leader but rather one associated with servants. Yet, in **John 13:4-5**, Jesus humbled Himself, taking a towel and washing the feet of those who followed Him. This gesture was more than an act of kindness; it was a profound example of love, teaching us that true greatness comes from choosing to serve others.

Through this act, Jesus shattered conventional ideas about leadership and status. He reminded us that true leaders lift others up, rather than placing themselves above them. In **John 13:14-15,** Jesus said, "Now that I, your Lord and Teacher, have washed your feet, you also should wash one another's feet." This is a lesson for anyone aspiring to greatness: it is not achieved through titles or power but through selfless acts of love and care for others.

Greatness also means putting the needs of others above our own. Washing the disciples' feet was not just a physical act but a symbol of humility and a call to action. Jesus demonstrated that those who truly want to make a difference must be willing to perform even the simplest tasks in service to others. It is through small, thoughtful actions that we build trust, respect, and deep, meaningful connections.

This story encourages us to live with purpose and humility every day. Greatness is not about fame or recognition; it is about leaving an impact on others' lives through kindness and service. If we embrace this lesson, we can lead by example, inspire others, and create a legacy of love and humility that reflects the greatness Jesus modeled for us.

2. Welcome Sinners and Everybody

Jesus showed extraordinary humility by welcoming everyone, including sinners and outcasts, with compassion and love. He did not judge people by their past or social status, but embraced them with kindness. In **Matthew 9:10-11**, we see Him eating with tax collectors and sinners, an act that challenged societal norms and demonstrated His deep care for those who were often rejected. By welcoming all, Jesus teaches us the power of humility and acceptance, reminding us to see people for who they are and not where they come from.

This act of openness gives us important lessons for achieving greatness. First, true greatness comes from humility—it's about lifting others up instead of looking down on them. Second, we must embrace people with kindness, regardless of their background, showing them they are valued. Third, greatness involves serving those in need, just as Jesus did when He sought out and supported those who were lost. Fourth, we learn that showing love and compassion to everyone, even those society may overlook, builds stronger, more meaningful connections. Fifth, greatness means setting aside judgment and creating a space of inclusivity where all feel welcome and supported.

Jesus' actions inspire us to lead our lives with humility and love. Greatness is not about fame or titles—it is found in how we treat others and the impact we have on their lives. If we practice acceptance, kindness, and service, we can follow His example and create a life filled with purpose, compassion, and meaningful relationships. Let His example guide us to live with humility and to embrace the greatness that comes from loving others unconditionally.

3. Worship

True greatness begins with a heart of humility, as Jesus showed through His worship and devotion to God. He often withdrew to quiet places to pray, seeking not His own will but the will of the Father. In **Luke 5:16**, it is written, *"But Jesus often withdrew to* *lonely places and prayed."* This devotion demonstrates that true worship is about acknowledging our dependence on God and prioritizing our relationship with Him. By humbling Himself in prayer, Jesus showed that greatness starts with surrendering our will to align with God's perfect plan.

Jesus also teaches us that humility in worship brings honor from God. In **John 4:23**, He said, *"True worshipers will worship the Father in the Spirit and in truth, for they are the kind of worshipers the Father seeks."* When we humble ourselves and seek God with a sincere heart, He honors us with guidance, strength, and purpose. This shows that greatness is not achieved by exalting ourselves but by exalting God, trusting Him to lift us up in His time and way.

Through Jesus' example, we learn four key lessons about worship that lead to greatness. First, worship calls us to surrender our will and trust God's plan. Second, true humility opens the door to God's blessings and wisdom. Third, consistent prayer keeps us connected to God's strength and guidance. Lastly, honoring God in all we do inspires us to lead lives of purpose and compassion. By following Jesus' example, we can embrace humility and discover the greatness that comes from a life devoted to God.

4. Work with Others

Jesus showed us that true greatness comes from working together and valuing others' contributions. He demonstrated this through His relationship with His twelve disciples, whom He chose to assist Him in spreading His message. In **Mark 3:14**, it says, *"He appointed twelve that they might be with him and that he might send them out to preach."* By teaching and empowering them, Jesus showed the importance of recognizing the strengths of those around us and supporting them in their purpose. His actions remind us that greatness is built through collaboration and shared effort.

SYAVIHA MULENGYA

From Jesus' example, we can learn five key lessons about greatness. First, humility allows us to appreciate and respect what others bring to the table. Second, empowering those around us helps create stronger connections and shared success. Third, working together nurtures unity and trust among people. Fourth, we should strive to uplift and encourage others, building an environment of positivity and growth. Finally, greatness lies in seeing those we work with as partners and friends, not as subordinates, just as Jesus did when He said, "*I no longer call you servants... Instead, I have called you friends*" (**John 15:15**). By embracing these lessons, we can achieve greatness through humility, collaboration, and love.

5. Witness

Jesus showed that true greatness comes from humility and selflessness. He devoted His life to witnessing to others, sharing God's message of love and salvation. **Matthew 4:23** says, "*Jesus went throughout Galilee, teaching in their synagogues, proclaiming the good news of the kingdom, and healing every disease and sickness among the people.*" His actions remind us that humility means putting the needs of others before our own, spreading kindness, and giving hope to those around us.

From Jesus' example, we learn three important lessons about greatness. First, true greatness comes from serving others with compassion and understanding. Second, selflessness opens the door to making a meaningful difference in others' lives. Third, sharing love and truth freely builds trust and inspires others to grow. As Jesus said in **Matthew 28:19-20**, "*Go and make disciples of all nations... teaching them to obey everything I have commanded you.*" By following these lessons, we can learn to live with purpose and bring positive change to the world.

SYAVIHA MULENGYA

11

Forgiveness Brings Hope, Healing, And Harmony

Forgiveness is a powerful gift that frees the heart and restores peace. When we choose to forgive, we let go of anger, bitterness, and pain—and make room for healing to begin. The Bible says, *"Bear with each other and forgive one another… Forgive as the Lord forgave you"* (**Colossians 3:13**). Forgiveness doesn't mean forgetting the hurt or pretending it didn't happen— it means releasing the burden and trusting God to bring justice and peace. It brings hope because it opens the door to new beginnings. It brings healing because it softens the wounds of the past. And it brings harmony by rebuilding broken relationships and restoring unity. Whether we forgive others or ourselves, we step into freedom. Jesus showed us this on the cross when He said, *"Father, forgive them"* (**Luke 23:34**). That kind of love changes everything. When we forgive, we reflect God's grace—and that grace brings peace to our souls and harmony to our lives.

SYAVIHA MULENGYA

A Humble Person Forgives

A humble person forgives because they understand that holding on to pain only makes it worse. Forgiveness sets you free— it lifts the heavy burden of anger, hurt, and bitterness from your heart. When you forgive, you stop carrying the weight of the past and start walking in peace. It doesn't mean the wrong never happened—it means you choose healing over revenge. Forgiveness also helps solve the problem. It opens the door to honest conversations, healing, and restoration. Instead of staying stuck in conflict, forgiveness moves things forward. A humble heart sees the need for unity. It knows that relationships matter more than being right. Forgiveness brings people together, breaks down walls, and builds bridges. It strengthens your spirit and your relationships. It makes you wiser, kinder, and more like Christ.

Forgiveness also silences the voice of pride. Pride wants to fight, blame, and stay angry. But humility says, "I'm sorry," or "I forgive you," and peace follows. Forgiveness settles the storm inside. It soothes the pain, calms the emotions, and brings comfort to the soul. It shields your heart from becoming bitter or cold. When you forgive, you protect your joy, your peace, and your future. A humble person doesn't wait for the perfect apology—they choose grace. They know that forgiveness is not weakness—it's strength. Jesus forgave those who hurt Him, and He calls us to do the same. Forgiveness is a gift you give to others, but also to yourself. It brings freedom, unity, and healing. And it always walks hand in hand with humility.

1. Sets Free

Forgiveness sets you free from the prison of pain and bitterness. When you hold on to anger, it quietly controls your thoughts, emotions, and even your future. A humble person understands that freedom doesn't come from revenge—it comes from release. Letting go of the offense doesn't mean it didn't hurt; it means you won't let it hold you hostage anymore. Forgiveness lifts the weight off your shoulders and gives your heart room to breathe. It allows you to walk forward without dragging the past behind you. You stop replaying the moment and start reclaiming your peace. Jesus said, *"So if the Son sets you free, you will be free indeed"* (**John 8:36**), and forgiveness is one way that freedom becomes real in your life. A humble heart knows that freedom is more valuable than pride. Forgiveness is not weakness—it's strength in motion. It's the decision to live light, not heavy. And in that choice, you find freedom that pride could never offer.

Freedom also shows up in your relationships. When you forgive, you stop punishing others for what someone else did. You stop building walls and start building bridges. A humble person doesn't need to win—they want to grow. Forgiveness clears the air and opens the door to new beginnings. It allows love to flow again where bitterness once lived. You become easier to talk to, easier to trust, and easier to love. Forgiveness frees you from being stuck in the past and helps you focus on what's ahead. It gives you emotional clarity and spiritual strength. You stop being defined by your wounds and start being shaped by grace. A humble heart forgives because it wants peace more than power. And that peace becomes the foundation for a life of joy, purpose, and connection.

2. Solves the Problem

Forgiveness is often the first step toward solving a deeper problem. A humble person doesn't ignore conflict—they face it with grace and courage. Pride says, "Stay angry," but humility says, "Let's fix this." When you forgive, you open the door to honest conversations and healing. You allow space for understanding, not just reaction. Forgiveness doesn't erase the issue, but it makes resolution possible. It softens hearts and clears the way for truth. The Bible says, *"Bear with each other and forgive one another if any of you has a grievance against someone. Forgive as the Lord forgave you"* (**Colossians 3:13**), reminding us that forgiveness is a divine tool for restoration. A humble heart doesn't need to win—it wants to grow. Forgiveness helps people see each other clearly again. It removes the fog of offense and brings clarity to the situation. And with clarity comes the chance to rebuild what was broken.

Solving problems through forgiveness builds trust and emotional safety. When you forgive, you show others that love is stronger than mistakes. You create space for growth, not guilt. A humble heart doesn't hold grudges—it holds grace. Forgiveness turns conflict into connection. It allows people to move forward without dragging the past into every conversation. You stop keeping score and start keeping peace. Forgiveness is not the end—it's the beginning of healing. It invites both sides to listen, learn, and grow. A humble person forgives because they want unity, not division. They know that problems don't disappear—they're solved through love. And love always starts with forgiveness.

3. Sees the Need for Unity

A humble person forgives because they understand the value of unity. They know that relationships matter more than pride or being right. Forgiveness brings people together—it heals broken bonds and restores trust. When you forgive, you choose connection over separation. You say, "We're better together than apart." Unity doesn't mean perfect agreement—it means shared purpose and mutual respect. A humble heart values peace more than control. Forgiveness keeps families close, friendships strong, and communities healthy. It's the glue that holds relationships together. Without forgiveness, small offenses grow into big walls. But with forgiveness, those walls come down. And when walls fall, unity rises.

Unity also brings strength and safety. When people are united, they can overcome anything. Forgiveness is the bridge that makes unity possible. A humble person doesn't let pride block that bridge. They choose to forgive so that love can flow freely. The Bible says, *"Make every effort to keep the unity of the Spirit through the bond of peace"* (**Ephesians 4:3**), reminding us that unity is worth fighting for. Unity creates trust, joy, and purpose. It allows people to work together, dream together, and grow together. Forgiveness is the foundation of that unity. It says, "I care more about us than about my ego." A humble heart forgives because it wants to build, not break. And through forgiveness, unity becomes a reality.

4. Strengthens

Forgiveness strengthens your heart in ways pride never can. A humble person knows that forgiving doesn't make you weak—it makes you wiser. It takes courage to let go of hurt and choose peace. That courage builds emotional and spiritual strength. When you forgive, you grow in patience, grace, and resilience. You learn to love deeper and live freer. Forgiveness stretches your heart and teaches you how to handle pain with purpose. It makes you stronger because you've chosen healing over revenge. A humble heart doesn't need to win—it wants to grow. Strength isn't just about standing tall—it's about standing true. The Bible says, *"Be kind and compassionate to one another, forgiving each other, just as in Christ God forgave you"* (**Ephesians 4:32**). Forgiveness helps you stand firm in love, even when others fall short.

Forgiveness also strengthens relationships. It rebuilds trust and restores connection. When you forgive, you show others that love is stronger than mistakes. You create space for honesty, growth, and healing. A humble person forgives because they want relationships that last. They know that holding grudges only weakens the bond. Forgiveness makes relationships more durable, more meaningful, and more joyful. It teaches people how to love through the hard times. It shows that grace is more powerful than pride. A strong relationship isn't perfect—it's built on forgiveness. A humble heart forgives because it wants to build, not break. And in that building, strength is multiplied.

5. Silences

Forgiveness silences the voice of pride, anger, and revenge. It quiets the noise that keeps your heart in turmoil. A humble person forgives because they don't need to prove anything. They choose peace over drama, healing over hostility. Forgiveness says, "I won't let this pain speak louder than love." It silences the urge to fight back and replaces it with grace. Pride wants to shout, but humility listens. Forgiveness brings quiet strength that doesn't need applause. It calms the storm inside and brings clarity to your thoughts. The Bible says, *"Refrain from anger and turn from wrath; do not fret—it leads only to evil"* (**Psalm 37:8**), reminding us that silence can be holy. A humble heart doesn't shout—it speaks softly with wisdom. And when you turn down the noise, you can finally hear peace.

It also silences the lies that pride tells. Pride says, "You're weak if you forgive," but humility knows the truth. Forgiveness is not weakness—it's wisdom in action. It silences the bitterness that tries to take root. It quiets the fear that says, "They'll hurt you again." A humble person forgives because they trust God more than their pain. They know that silence can be powerful when filled with grace. Forgiveness doesn't need to be loud—it needs to be real. It replaces shouting with serenity. It turns conflict into calm. A humble heart forgives because it wants peace to speak louder than pride. And in that silence, healing begins.

6. Settles and Soothes

"Let the peace of Christ rule in your hearts, since as members of one body you were called to peace." — **Colossians 3:15**

Forgiveness settles the storm inside your heart. It brings calm where there was once chaos and confusion. A humble person forgives because they want peace, not power. Forgiveness settles arguments, eases tension, and restores emotional balance. It's like a gentle breeze after a long storm—it doesn't erase the damage, but it helps you breathe again. When you forgive, you stop feeding the fire of anger and start watering the soil of healing. You allow grace to take the lead instead of pride. The Bible says, *"Let the peace of Christ rule in your hearts, since as members of one body you were called to peace"* (**Colossians 3:15**), reminding us that peace is our calling. A humble heart doesn't stir conflict—it settles it with love. Forgiveness is the quiet answer to loud pain. It brings rest to restless minds and comfort to wounded souls. And in that settling, peace finds a permanent home.

Forgiveness also soothes the emotions that pride inflames. Pride keeps wounds open, but humility helps them heal. A humble person forgives because they want comfort, not control. Forgiveness is a balm for the soul—it cools the heat of anger and eases the sting of offense. It brings emotional relief and spiritual refreshment. You stop replaying the hurt and start receiving peace. Forgiveness soothes the heart like a gentle touch. It reminds you that grace is stronger than pain. A humble heart doesn't hold on— it lets go with love. The Bible teaches, *"A gentle answer turns away wrath, but a harsh word stirs up anger"* (**Proverbs 15:1**), showing that softness brings healing. Forgiveness is the medicine that pride refuses but humility embraces. And in that soothing, strength is restored.

7. Shields

"Above all else, guard your heart, for everything you do flows from it." — **Proverbs 4:23**

Forgiveness shields your heart from bitterness and your relationships from destruction. A humble person forgives because they know that holding on to hurt only causes more damage. Forgiveness is a form of protection—it guards your peace, your joy, and your future. It keeps your heart soft and your spirit strong. Pride opens the door to resentment, but humility builds a wall of grace. Forgiveness is the shield that blocks bitterness from taking root. It protects your mind from toxic thoughts and your soul from spiritual decay. The Bible says, *"Above all else, guard your heart, for everything you do flows from it"* (**Proverbs 4:23**), reminding us that forgiveness is part of guarding what matters most. A humble heart forgives because it wants to stay whole. Forgiveness is not just a reaction—it's a defense. It keeps you from becoming the very thing that hurt you. And in that protection, you find peace.

Forgiveness also shields others from your pain. When you forgive, you stop spreading hurt and start spreading healing. A humble person forgives because they want to protect what matters most. They know that love is worth guarding. Forgiveness shields relationships from falling apart. It keeps families together, friendships strong, and communities united. It's a covering of grace that holds people close. A humble heart doesn't seek revenge—it seeks restoration. The Bible says, *"Hatred stirs up conflict, but love covers over all wrongs"* (**Proverbs 10:12**), showing that forgiveness is love in action. Forgiveness is a shelter from the storm of pride.

It's not just a soft response—it's a strong shield. And when you forgive, you protect your heart and the hearts of those around you.

12

Pride Is Not For People like You

Sources of Pride

1. Ingratitude

Ingratitude is a source of pride. When you fail to appreciate the blessings and kindness you receive, you may start to believe that you deserve everything you have without acknowledging the contributions of others. This attitude can lead to arrogance and a sense of entitlement. **Romans 1:21** says, *"For although they knew God, they neither glorified him as God nor gave thanks to him, but their thinking became futile and their foolish hearts were darkened."* Ingratitude blinds you to the importance of humility and gratitude.

Ingratitude can damage relationships and create a negative environment. When you don't express gratitude, people may feel unappreciated and undervalued. This lack of appreciation can lead to resentment and conflict. By practicing humility and showing gratitude, you can foster positive relationships and create a supportive community. **1 Thessalonians 5:18** advises, *"Give thanks in all circumstances; for this is God's will for you in Christ Jesus."*

2. Insecurity

Insecurity is another source of pride. When you feel insecure, you may try to compensate by boasting about your achievements or belittling others to make yourself feel better. This behavior is driven by a need to prove your worth and can lead to arrogance. **Proverbs 29:23** says, *"Pride brings a person low, but the lowly in spirit gain honor."* Insecurity can prevent you from embracing humility and seeking genuine connections.

Insecurity can also hinder personal growth and self-improvement. When you are focused on proving yourself, you may resist feedback and avoid acknowledging your weaknesses. This attitude can prevent you from learning and growing. By practicing humility and addressing your insecurities, you can build confidence and foster positive relationships. **Psalm 139:14** reminds us, *"I praise you because I am fearfully and wonderfully made; your works are wonderful, I know that full well."*

3. Ignorance

Ignorance is a source of pride. When you lack knowledge or understanding, you may become arrogant and dismissive of others' opinions and experiences. This attitude can lead to poor decision-making and conflict. **Proverbs 12:15** says, *"The way of fools seems right to them, but the wise listen to advice."* Ignorance can prevent you from embracing humility and seeking wisdom.

Ignorance can also create barriers to personal growth and development. When you are unwilling to learn and expand your knowledge, you limit your potential and miss out on valuable opportunities. By practicing humility and seeking knowledge, you can overcome ignorance and achieve greater success. Proverbs 18:15 advises, "The heart of the discerning acquires knowledge, for the ears of the wise seek it out."

4. Impression

The desire to impress others is a source of pride. When you focus on creating a certain image or gaining approval, you may become arrogant and self-centered. This behavior can lead to superficial relationships and a lack of genuine connections. **Galatians 1:10** says, *"Am I now trying to win the approval of human beings, or of God? Or am I trying to please people? If I were still trying to please people, I would not be a servant of Christ."* The need to impress others can prevent you from embracing humility and authenticity.

The desire to impress can also lead to stress and anxiety. When you are constantly trying to meet others' expectations, you may feel overwhelmed and insecure. By practicing humility and focusing on genuine relationships, you can reduce stress and build meaningful connections. **Proverbs 29:25** advises, *"Fear of man will prove to be a snare, but whoever trusts in the Lord is kept safe."*

5. Imitation

Imitation is a source of pride. When you try to imitate others to fit in or gain approval, you may lose sight of your true self and become arrogant. This behavior can lead to a lack of authenticity and genuine connections. **Romans 12:2** says, *"Do not conform to the pattern of this world, but be transformed by the renewing of your mind."* Imitation can prevent you from embracing humility and being true to yourself.

Imitation can also hinder personal growth and self-discovery. When you focus on copying others, you may miss out on opportunities to develop your unique strengths and talents. By practicing humility and embracing your individuality, you can achieve greater success and build genuine relationships. **Galatians 6:4** advises, *"Each one should test their own actions. Then they can take pride in themselves alone, without comparing themselves to someone else."*

6. Inferiority

Feelings of inferiority can be a source of pride. When you feel inferior, you may try to compensate by boasting or belittling others to make yourself feel better. This behavior is driven by a need to prove your worth and can lead to arrogance. **Proverbs 16:18** says, *"Pride goes before destruction, a haughty spirit before a fall."* Inferiority can prevent you from embracing humility and seeking genuine connections.

Feelings of inferiority can also hinder personal growth and self-improvement. When you are focused on proving yourself, you may resist feedback and avoid acknowledging your weaknesses. This attitude can prevent you from learning and growing. By practicing humility and addressing your feelings of inferiority, you can build confidence and foster positive relationships. **Psalm 139:14** reminds us, *"I praise you because I am fearfully and wonderfully made; your works are wonderful, I know that full well."*

How to Overcome Pride

1. Check Yourself

To overcome pride, start by checking yourself. Reflect on your thoughts and actions to identify any signs of pride. Ask yourself whether you are acting out of arrogance or putting yourself above others. **Proverbs 21:2** says, *"A person may think their own ways are* *right, but the Lord weighs the heart."* Self-reflection helps you recognize areas where pride may be affecting your behavior.

Checking yourself involves being honest about your motivations and attitudes. It means acknowledging when you are wrong and being willing to change. This honesty is the first step towards humility. **Psalm 139:23-24** advises, *"Search me, God, and know my heart; test me and know my anxious thoughts. See if there is any offensive way in me, and lead me in the way everlasting."* By regularly checking yourself, you can stay aware of pride and work towards overcoming it.

Checking yourself also means seeking feedback from others. Ask trusted friends or family members to help you identify areas where pride may be influencing your actions. Their insights can provide valuable perspectives and help you grow. **Proverbs 27:17** says, *"As iron sharpens iron, so one person sharpens another."* By being open to feedback, you can better understand and address pride in your life.

2. Correct Your Behavior

Once you have identified areas of pride, take steps to correct your behavior. This involves making conscious efforts to act with humility and kindness. **Philippians 2:3-4** advises, *"Do nothing out of selfish ambition or vain conceit. Rather, in humility value others above yourselves, not looking to your own interests but each of you to the interests of the others."* Correcting your behavior helps you develop a humble attitude.

Correcting your behavior means being mindful of how you treat others. Show respect and appreciation for their contributions, and avoid belittling or dismissing their opinions. This approach fosters positive relationships and creates a supportive environment.

Ephesians 4:2 says, *"Be completely humble and gentle; be patient, bearing with one another in love."* By treating others with kindness, you can overcome pride and build stronger connections.

Correcting your behavior also involves making amends when you have acted out of pride. Apologize to those you may have hurt and seek forgiveness. This act of humility helps repair relationships and demonstrates your commitment to change. **James 5:16** advises, *"Therefore confess your sins to each other and pray for each other so that you may be healed."* By taking responsibility for your actions, you can overcome pride and foster healing.

3. Choose to Trust God

Overcoming pride requires choosing to trust God. Recognize that you cannot do everything on your own and that you need His guidance and strength. **Proverbs 3:5-6** says, *"Trust in the Lord with all your heart and lean not on your own understanding; in all your ways submit to him, and he will make your paths straight."* Trusting God helps you develop humility and reliance on His wisdom.

Choosing to trust God means seeking His will in your decisions and actions. Pray for guidance and be open to His direction. This trust helps you let go of pride and embrace humility. **Psalm 37:5** advises, *"Commit your way to the Lord; trust in him and he will do this."* By relying on God, you can overcome pride and find peace in His plan for your life.

Trusting God also involves recognizing His sovereignty and greatness. Acknowledge that He is in control and that His ways are higher than yours. This recognition fosters humility and helps you stay grounded. Isaiah 55:8-9 says, *"For my thoughts are not your thoughts, neither are your ways my ways,"* declares the Lord. *"As the heavens are higher than the earth, so are my ways higher than your ways and my thoughts than your thoughts."* By choosing to trust God, you can overcome pride and experience His blessings.

4. Count on God

Counting on God is essential for overcoming pride. Depend on Him for strength, wisdom, and guidance in all aspects of your life. **Philippians 4:13** says, *"I can do all this through him who gives me strength."* Counting on God helps you recognize your limitations and develop humility.

Counting on God means seeking His help in times of need. Pray for His support and trust that He will provide. This dependence fosters a humble attitude and helps you let go of pride. **Psalm 46:1** says, *"God is our refuge and strength, an ever-present help in trouble."* By relying on God, you can overcome pride and find comfort in His presence.

Counting on God also involves acknowledging His role in your successes and achievements. Give Him credit for the blessings in your life and recognize that they come from Him. This gratitude fosters humility and helps you stay grounded. **James 1:17** says, *"Every good and perfect gift is from above, coming down from the Father of the heavenly lights."* By counting on God, you can overcome pride and experience His grace.

5. Cultivate Gratitude

Cultivating gratitude is a powerful way to overcome pride. When you express gratitude, you acknowledge the contributions of others and the blessings in your life. **1 Thessalonians 5:18** says, *"Give thanks in all circumstances; for this is God's will for you in Christ Jesus."* Gratitude helps you develop humility and appreciation.

Cultivating gratitude involves regularly reflecting on the good things in your life and expressing thanks. This practice shifts your focus away from yourself and towards the positive aspects of life. **Philippians 4:6-7** advises, *"Do not be anxious about anything, but in every situation, by prayer and petition, with thanksgiving, present your requests to God."* By practicing gratitude, you can overcome pride and experience greater contentment.

Gratitude also fosters positive relationships. When you express appreciation for others, they feel valued and respected. This sense of appreciation strengthens the bond between you and creates a supportive environment. **Colossians 3:15** says, *"Let the peace of Christ rule in your hearts, since as members of one body you were called to peace. And be thankful."* By cultivating gratitude, you can overcome pride and build stronger connections.

6. Celebrate Others

Celebrating others is a sign of humility. When you acknowledge and appreciate the achievements and strengths of those around you, you show that you value their contributions. **Romans 12:10** says, *"Be devoted to one another in love. Honor one another above yourselves."* Celebrating others helps you develop a humble attitude and build positive relationships.

Celebrating others involves recognizing their efforts and expressing genuine admiration. This practice fosters a sense of community and mutual respect. **Philippians 2:3** advises, *"Do nothing out of selfish ambition or vain conceit. Rather, in humility value others above yourselves."* By celebrating others, you can overcome pride and create a supportive environment.

Celebrating others also means being happy for their successes without envy or jealousy. It requires a selfless attitude and a genuine desire to see others thrive. **Proverbs 27:17** says, *"As iron sharpens iron, so one person sharpens another."* By practicing humility and celebrating others, you can overcome pride and build meaningful connections.

13

Manage Well What You Have

Don't Waste What You Carry

There was once a doctor who was a highly skilled specialist in his field. Despite his expertise, he didn't care much for his patients. He would treat them when and how he wanted, often ignoring their needs. If he didn't like someone, he would send them away, asking them to come another day. He regularly missed appointments without giving any notice, frustrating both patients and staff. The hospital manager tried to correct him many times, but the doctor became even more arrogant. He started skipping work, and one day, knowing that over 30 patients were booked to see him, he went on vacation without informing anyone. When the manager called him to ask how he could leave so suddenly, the doctor arrogantly replied, "I'm on vacation. Deal with it."

While the specialist was away, a young trainee stepped in to help. The trainee worked hard, showing great care and dedication to the patients. He treated each one with kindness and respect, making sure no one was left unattended. The manager was impressed, realizing that this young man had done what the specialist never could—he provided excellent care and made the patients feel valued. Word quickly spread, and the trainee gained a reputation for being compassionate and skilled.

When the specialist returned, he confidently declared, "I'm back. I'm here to reclaim my job." But the manager told him there was no place for him anymore. Angry and full of pride, the specialist scoffed, "You think you can manage without me?" The manager firmly replied, "We will manage." The trainee officially took over the position, and under his care, the center became well-known for its exceptional service. Patients flocked to see him, and he helped many sick people find healing.

One day, someone asked the young man how he was able to do such amazing work. He humbly replied, "This must be God. I always start with prayer and end with prayer." Meanwhile, the proud specialist became bitter and broke. He lost everything because of his arrogance. His pride had blinded him to the importance of humility and gratitude, and it cost him dearly.

This story teaches an important lesson about pride. Pride can make us think we are better than others and that we don't need anyone's help. It can blind us to the value of humility and make us miss out on the best opportunities in life. As the Bible warns in **Proverbs 16:18**, *"Pride goes before destruction, a haughty spirit before a fall."* What we have is small compared to what God has in store for us, and we need to manage our blessings with humility.

Managing blessings means staying humble, no matter how great our achievements or possessions may be. It's about recognizing that God is the source of all our blessings and giving Him the glory. We are blessed to be a blessing to others, not to boast or feel superior. Never forget where you came from or who helped you along the way. Humility helps us remain grounded and grateful.

I've seen talented people let pride get in the way of their relationships and responsibilities. For example, I once worked with a musician who gave the church a hard time because he thought his talent made him indispensable. He believed that without him, nothing would work well. This kind of attitude only creates tension and isolates people.

True humility involves understanding the source of your blessings and practicing gratitude. Say "thank you" often—to God and to those who support you. Stay connected to your values and remember that your blessings are not just for your benefit. Share what you have, serve others, and surround yourself with grounded, humble people.

Humility allows us to appreciate what we have and use it for good. It reminds us that success is not about being better than others but about using our blessings wisely. Gratitude and humility lead to greater joy and satisfaction, while pride can only bring emptiness and loss.

As the trainee in the story showed, humility opens the door to greatness. By putting others first and giving credit to God, he became a blessing to many people. Let this story remind us to stay humble, give thanks, and use our blessings to help others. Only then can we truly enjoy the gifts we have been given.

Manage well The Following;

1. Achievement

Achievements can lead to pride if not managed well. When you accomplish something significant, it's natural to feel proud, but it's important to stay humble and recognize the contributions of others. **Proverbs 16:18** warns, *"Pride goes before destruction, a haughty spirit before a fall."* Acknowledging the support and guidance you received helps you stay grounded.

Managing achievements involves giving credit where it's due and expressing gratitude. Celebrate your success, but also appreciate the efforts of those who helped you along the way. This attitude leads to humility and strengthens relationships. **Philippians 2:3** advises, *"Do nothing out of selfish ambition or vain conceit. Rather, in humility value others above yourselves."* Reflect on your achievements and identify the people who contributed to your success. Take time to thank them and acknowledge their support. This practice helps you stay humble and avoid the pitfalls of pride.

2. Asset

Assets, such as wealth and possessions, can lead to pride if not managed well. When you have valuable assets, it's easy to feel superior or entitled. However, it's important to remember that everything you have is a blessing from God. **Proverbs 11:28** says, *"Those who trust in their riches will fall, but the righteous will thrive like a green leaf."* Recognizing God's provision helps you stay humble.

Managing assets involves using them wisely and generously. Share your blessings with others and avoid flaunting your wealth. This approach fosters humility and has a positive impact on those around you. **1 Timothy 6:17-18** advises, *"Command those who are rich in this present world not to be arrogant nor to put their hope in wealth... Command them to do good, to be rich in good deeds, and to be generous and willing to share."* Evaluate how you use your assets and find ways to share your blessings with others. This practice helps you stay humble and avoid the pitfalls of pride.

3. Award

Awards and recognition can lead to pride if not managed well. When you receive an award, it's natural to feel proud, but it's important to stay humble and acknowledge the contributions of others. **Proverbs 27:2** advises, *"Let someone else praise you, and not your own mouth; an outsider, and not your own lips."* Recognizing the support and guidance you received helps you stay grounded.

Managing awards involves expressing gratitude and giving credit where it's due. Celebrate your success, but also appreciate the efforts of those who helped you along the way. This attitude fosters humility and strengthens relationships. **Romans 12:10** says, *"Be devoted to one another in love. Honor one another above yourselves."*

Reflect on the awards you have received and identify the people who contributed to your success. Take time to thank them and acknowledge their support. This practice helps you stay humble and avoid the pitfalls of pride.

4. Appearance

Appearance can lead to pride if not managed well. When you focus too much on your looks, you may become vain or arrogant. It's important to remember that true beauty comes from within. **1 Samuel 16:7** says, *"The Lord does not look at the things people look at. People look at the outward appearance, but the Lord looks at the heart."* Recognizing the importance of inner beauty helps you stay humble.

Managing appearance involves focusing on your character and actions rather than just your looks. Cultivate qualities like kindness, compassion, and humility. This approach facilitates genuine connections and creates a positive impact on those around you. **Proverbs 31:30** advises, *"Charm is deceptive, and beauty is fleeting; but a woman who fears the Lord is to be praised."* Reflect on how you present yourself and focus on developing your inner qualities. This practice helps you stay humble and avoid the pitfalls of pride.

5. Admiration

Admiration from others can lead to pride if not managed well. When people praise you, it's easy to feel superior or entitled. However, it's important to stay humble and recognize that admiration is a reflection of God's blessings in your life. **Proverbs 27:21** says, *"The crucible for silver and the furnace for gold, but people are tested by their praise."* Recognizing God's role in your success helps you stay grounded.

Managing admiration involves expressing gratitude and giving credit where it's due. Appreciate the praise, but also acknowledge the contributions of others and God's blessings. This attitude influences humility and strengthens relationships. **James 4:10** advises, *"Humble yourselves before the Lord, and he will lift you up."* Reflect on the admiration you receive and find ways to express gratitude and acknowledge others' support. This practice helps you stay humble and avoid the pitfalls of pride.

6. Address

Your address or social status can lead to pride if not managed well. When you live in a prestigious area or have a high social status, it's easy to feel superior or entitled. However, it's important to remember that true worth comes from your character and actions.

Proverbs 22:1 says, "*A good name is more desirable than great riches; to be esteemed is better than silver or gold.*" Recognizing the importance of character helps you stay humble.

Managing your address involves focusing on your actions and how you treat others rather than just your social status. Cultivate qualities like kindness, compassion, and humility. This approach fosters genuine connections and creates a positive impact on those around you. **Romans 12:16** advises, "*Live in harmony with one another. Do not be proud, but be willing to associate with people of low position.*"

Reflect on how you view your social status and focus on developing your character. This practice helps you stay humble and avoid the pitfalls of pride.

7. Ambition

Ambition can lead to pride if not managed well. When you are driven to achieve your goals, it's easy to become arrogant or self-centered. However, it's important to stay humble and recognize that true success comes from God's blessings. **Proverbs 16:3** says, "*Commit to the Lord whatever you do, and he will establish your plans.*" Recognizing God's role in your success helps you stay grounded.

Managing ambition involves setting goals that align with God's will and seeking His guidance. Stay focused on your purpose and avoid becoming obsessed with personal achievements. This approach fosters humility and creates a positive impact on those around you. **Philippians 2:3** advises, "*Do nothing out of selfish ambition or vain conceit. Rather, in humility value others above yourselves.*"

Reflect on your ambitions and ensure they align with God's will. Seek His guidance and stay focused on your purpose. This practice helps you stay humble and avoid the pitfalls of pride.

Prayer for Humility

Heavenly Father, I come before You with a quiet heart, asking for Your help. Teach me to walk in humility, not pride. Help me to see others through Your eyes—with love, grace, and compassion. Remove any selfishness or arrogance from my spirit. Let me be quick to listen, slow to speak, and gentle in my actions. Remind me that greatness comes from serving, not being served. Just as Jesus humbled Himself, help me to follow His example. Give me the strength to admit when I'm wrong and the courage to say "I'm sorry." Let my heart be soft, my words be kind, and my spirit be teachable. May I never think of myself more highly than I ought, but always honor You in how I treat others. Fill me with Your peace and wisdom, and help me to live with a humble heart every day. In Jesus' name, Amen.

Prayer for Repentance

Lord God, I come to You with a heart that needs healing. I confess my sins and ask for Your mercy. Forgive me for the times I've turned away from You, for the words I've spoken, and the choices I've made that didn't honor You. Cleanse me from all unrighteousness and renew a right spirit within me. I'm sorry for the hurt I've caused—to You, to others, and even to myself. I don't want to carry guilt or shame anymore. Your Word says, *"If we confess our sins, You are faithful and just to forgive us"* (**1 John 1:9**), and I hold on to that promise. Restore my joy, renew my mind, and lead me in Your truth. Help me to walk in obedience and love. Give me the strength to turn away from sin and the grace to walk in freedom. Thank You for Your forgiveness, Your patience, and Your unfailing love. In Jesus' name, Amen.

By SYAVIHA MULENGYA

www.ingramcontent.com/pod-product-compliance
Lightning Source LLC
Chambersburg PA
CBHW061807120626
46550CB00005B/2172